Missing Millions

how abortion is harming us all

Edited by

Lynda Rose

VOICE FOR JUSTICE UK

Published in Great Britain in 2021 by
Voice for Justice UK
PO Box 8893 OX1 9PY

Unless otherwise indicated, scripture quotations are taken from the HOLY BIBLE, English Standard Version (ESV), Revised Standard Version (RSV), New International Version (NIV). Copyright © 1973, 1978, 1984 by International Bible Society. Used by permission.

Voice for Justice UK works to uphold and defend human rights, and to be a voice for those who cannot speak for themselves. Interested readers are invited to consult the website for details of its activities at
www.vfjuk.org.uk

Voice for Justice UK

ISBN 978-0-9929964-3-7

Printed in Great Britain by Imprint Digital, Exeter

Commendations

The Duchess of Sussex has recently written of her sadness at suffering a miscarriage and the publicity has been welcomed by some. At the same time some argue strongly to strengthen the legislation authorising abortion. This demonstrates a deep division of approach to this highly important topic, the relationship between a pregnant woman and the embryo she is carrying. There is also a question about research: up to what stage of an embryo's development should research using that embryo be permitted?

These issues merit informed debate. Considerable literature exists setting out different points of view. This book is a clear statement of one point of view, from authors authoritative in their fields, and I commend it to all who seek to take a wise view of this matter.

The Rt Hon Lord Mackay of Clashfern KT
Former Lord Chancellor

At a time when there is a desperate need for compassion and a social conscience, abortion hardens the heart and brutalises all those involved. This book raises important questions that society needs urgently to address.

Charlie Colchester
Former CEO and Co-founder of CARE

This timely and compelling book gives an overview of the current situation on abortion that enables the reader to gain a clear understanding of the issues involved. I warmly commend it.

The Revd Dr Clifford Hill MA, BD, PhD
Issachar Ministries

In America, 61 million babies – almost the entire population of the United Kingdom – have been aborted since 1973. This book is a timely warning and needs to be read around the world.

R.T. Kendall
Evangelist and author

Under current guidelines, would we have known Paralympic Gold Medallist Baroness Tanni Grey-Thompson, former Home Secretary Lord Blunkett, or high achiever against all odds, Baron Shinkwin? Quite possibly not, since the pressure on mothers to abort their unborn child scanned as disabled is intended to deny them life.

These are precious people, giving life, hope and strength to millions, disabled or not.

Who are we to destroy the unique blessing of life because we judge others to be potentially less perfect than ourselves? Please read this book; it's a real eye opener.

Baroness Nicholson of Winterbourne

Missing Millions is a must-read for all those serious about the consistent application of human rights to all human beings, including before birth. Each of the six chapters tackles a different aspect of the abortion debate – medical, legal, ethical, political and the practical care of vulnerable women. Every contribution provides food for thought and will challenge, provoke and inform. I commend Revd Lynda Rose for putting together such an excellent book. I am sure it will prove not just a vital resource for those already active in the pro-life movement, but also a valuable tool to use to reach out to people of good will who are still conflicted on the issue.

Professor David Paton
Professor of Industrial Economics
Nottingham University Business School

The numbers alone make a reconsideration of abortion in this country an imperative. Each one is a tragedy. This study I believe will help those with great responsibility for our public life see what is happening, and consider our response from medical, theological and pastoral points of view. May God show us what is taking place and what it is we are to do.

The Rt Revd Keith Sinclair
Former Bishop of Birkenhead

Biographies

The Revd Lynda Rose

Lynda Rose is an Anglican priest and writer. Called to the Bar in 1983, she subsequently went into Christian ministry and was among the first women in the UK to be ordained into the Anglican Church. She served in parish ministry in and around Oxford for a number of years, but increasingly felt called to campaign on pro-life and related Christian issues. Currently she is CEO of **Voice for Justice UK** and Executive Director of **ParentPower**; she also serves as Convenor of the Lords and Commons Family and Child Protection Group, a non-aligned Parliamentary research group. She is the author of several books for both the religious and general markets.

Professor John Wyatt

John Wyatt is Emeritus Professor of Neonatal Paediatrics, and was previously Professor of Ethics & Perinatology, at University College London. He was a senior researcher at the Faraday Institute for Science and Religion, Cambridge, until early 2019.

He is a doctor, author, speaker and research scientist. His background is as a consultant neonatologist and academic researcher, focusing on the mechanisms, treatment and prevention of brain damage in new-born infants. He is now engaged in addressing new ethical, philosophical and theological challenges caused by advances in medical science and technology.

Professor Wyatt worked as a paediatrician, specialising in the care of new-born babies, at a leading neonatal intensive care unit for more than 25 years. Through his clinical experience, he became increasingly aware of the ethical maelstrom caused by advancing technology, and the contentious debates about the nature of humanity at the beginning and end of life. He has previously served as a member of the Royal College of Physicians ethics committee. His website is: johnwyatt.com

Robert S. Harris

Robert S. Harris is Strategy Director of Voice of Justice UK and has served with the organisation since 2012. He has been a member of the Lords and Commons Family and Child Protection Group (LCFCPG) since 2011, and served as its Joint Convenor 2014-2019. His study, on what the scientific literature says about the adverse outcomes for women who have abortions, was published as part of a report produced by the LCFCPG, which he also jointly edited.

He is the author of an acclaimed book on same sex marriage, commended by public figures including Lord Mackay of Clashfern, the former Lord Chancellor. He has also contributed chapters to books dealing with education and religious liberty. Robert has been interviewed on television and radio, and has spoken at events in Parliament and elsewhere. He was the organiser of the pro-life conference held in late 2019 that led to the publication of *Missing Millions*.

Bishop Michael Nazir-Ali

Bishop Michael was the 106th Bishop of Rochester (1994-2009), and served as a member of the House of Lords (1999-2009). Originally from South-West Asia, where he served as Bishop of Raiwind in Pakistan, he was the first Diocesan Bishop in the Church of England born abroad. He was a member of the Human Fertilisation and Embryology Authority and Chair of its Ethics and Law Committee (1997-2003).

He read Economics, Sociology and Islamic History at the University of Karachi, and Theology at Fitzwilliam College and Ridley Hall, Cambridge. Bishop Michael has been a visiting lecturer at a number of universities and colleges in the UK, Canada, the USA and Australia, having also taught at colleges and universities in the UK and Pakistan. He is an Hon. Fellow of St Edmund Hall, Oxford and of Fitzwilliam College, Cambridge.

He is the author of twelve books, a number of monographs and reports, and numerous articles on faith and public life, freedom of belief, bioethics, the Anglican Communion, and relations with people of other faiths. Bishop Michael has served on a number of committees including the Archbishops' Council, and was Theological Consultant to the Crown Appointments Review Group (1998-2001). He has served on the board of Christian Aid and was a trustee of Traidcraft. In 2005 he was awarded the Paul Harris Fellowship by Rotary International. Bishop Michael is President of both the Network for Inter-Faith Concerns in the Anglican Communion, and the Oxford Centre for Training, Research, Advocacy and Dialogue (OXTRAD).

Andrew Stephenson

Andrew Stephenson is the founder and CEO of the Centre for Bio-Ethical Reform UK. He was previously a carpenter and furniture maker, before making the natural progression to social reform.

Clare McCullough

Clare grew up in an Irish Catholic family in London, where she learned that love of neighbour must be lived out concretely. After graduating in English from Royal Holloway, University of London, she met a group of Catholic Crisis Pregnancy Counsellors in Ireland, who were saving babies' lives and supporting their mothers; she was persuaded to open a similar centre in London. She has been running the Good Counsel Network for 23 years, working with a wonderful team of staff and volunteers who make their work possible. During that time, thousands of women have sought and received help from them to keep their babies. She has been voted Catholic Woman of the Year twice. Clare lives in London with her husband and son.

Textual note for the spellings of foetus/foetal or fetus/fetal

British dictionaries give the spellings "foetus" and "foetal", though the spellings "fetus" and "fetal" are etymologically correct, are used in the USA, and are preferred in medical writings. In Missing Millions, *the British form is the preferred spelling, but the American spelling is employed, where appropriate, in quotations and in Professor Wyatt's chapter detailing current medical practice.*

CONTENTS

FOREWORD

The Rt Hon Sir Jeffrey Donaldson MP

Back in 2008, my colleague Edward Leigh made what was, at the time, an astounding comment: that in modern Britain the most dangerous place to be was in your mother's womb. Since that time, the situation has become worse, so that now to be conceived is, for the individual, to be in a lottery, where the prize is birth, but the odds are heavily stacked against winning.

Figures released by the Office for National Statistics (ONS) in 2019 reveal that in the UK a quarter of all conceptions ended in abortion.[1] Yet even this highly concerning figure seems, for the abortion lobby, not to be enough, because activists are now campaigning not just for further liberalisation of current law, but for the unquestioned right of women to choose for themselves whether or not their child should be born. These are purely medical matters relating to reproductive health, campaigners argue, and as such should be outside the remit of the law.

We have already seen this enacted in Northern Ireland, with abortion now permitted on request and without cause up to 12 weeks. But the question is not, should we lift all restrictions as acknowledgment of a woman's right to choose what happens to her own body, but, have we as a society gone too far? To put it another way, is the falling birth rate adversely affecting the continuance of life in the UK today? Are the costs to society too high?

Every life is special, and every life – wanted or not – has a unique contribution to make. It is not far-fetched to say that when we reject, with barely a thought, the unique contributions of an unborn child, we are immeasurably impoverishing the future of humanity. But that is not the end of the story, because the cumulative loss of those lives has financial and cultural repercussions that, longer term, will affect the wellbeing of us all.

This book, compiled in large part from talks delivered at a conference in 2019, examines the hidden cost of what might accurately be described as the mass termination of the unborn, now exceeding 9 million since the 1967 Abortion Act. Some of the information and data will no doubt come to many as a surprise. But whether familiar or not, this information and data should give all of us pause for thought. Abortion is no longer simply an issue of morality or of women's rights: it has consequences that reach far into the future, affecting the fundamental composition of society and the economy. This book makes a valued contribution to the ongoing debate, and I unreservedly commend it to anyone who has ever wondered about the future of modern society, the justification for taking life, and at what point we recognise the enormous harm that abortion is doing.

Endnote

---

[1] https://assets.publishing.service.gov.uk/government/uploads/system/uploads/attachment_data/file/891405/abortion-statistics-commentary-2019.pdf

INTRODUCTION

The Revd Lynda Rose

"We want to stamp out the back-street abortions, but it is not the intention of the Promoters of the Bill to leave a wide open door for abortion on request."

So said David Steel MP in his speech to Parliament in 1966, when he introduced the Abortion Bill.[1] Throughout the long and bitter argument that followed, David Steel and advocates for the Bill were insistent that the proposed legislation was only a restrictive emergency measure, for women who would otherwise be driven to seek backstreet abortion. As such, it was predicted that it would be used infrequently, and only to provide proper care for women who would otherwise be at risk.

In the event, the Bill was passed on second reading by a resounding 223 votes to 29, but time has since shown just how naïve – one is tempted to say, disingenuous – were the arguments employed. The truth is that, since the passing of the Abortion Act on 27th October 1967, the UK has seen over 9,500,000 abortions, 98% of which were for what are euphemistically termed 'social reasons' – meaning that there is no justification for termination beyond the fact that the foetus is, for whatever reason, unwanted at the time. To break that down further, annually, England and Wales see around 200,000 abortions a year, but in 2020, between January and June, England and Wales had already recorded 109,836 abortions, the majority of which were self-administered, again under 'emergency' legislation – this time supposedly temporary – allowing women to access abortion provision online, and have the pills sent by post, during the coronavirus pandemic.[2] As a rider to that, according to recent figures released by the Office for National Statistics (ONS), a quarter of pregnancies in the UK now end in abortion.[3] The inescapable conclusion, therefore, is that, although access to abortion technically remains subject to law, in practice we now have abortion on request... with so many women 'requesting' it that it is not fanciful to say that many now see it as simply another form of contraception.

Does that matter? After all, the high numbers clearly indicate that there is a demand for such intervention and, at the end of the day, a woman has the right to decide what happens to her own body. Why should a woman have to play host to a parasite for nine months, the argument runs, if she doesn't want to? Her body, her choice! It's all a question of rights.

Whatever pro-abortion activists would have us believe, however, it is not as simple as that. For a start, in any planned abortion there are two sets of *rights* to be considered, the woman's and the child's, though the right to life of the unborn child – who, in the absence of maternal defence, lacks an advocate – is largely overlooked or discounted. Secondly, for a woman, the decision to abort her child is both difficult and costly. Fuelled by hormones, a mother's every instinct is to protect and cherish the new life growing in her womb, so that the loss of that child inevitably leaves pain and distress. And, despite the argument put forward by abortion providers that termination is simply the removal of a problem, for some the pain of guilt and loss will never go away, colouring the whole of the rest of that woman's life. In fact, no matter what is maintained by abortion providers, the truth is that many women, post abortion, experience depression and mental health problems. Many never forgive themselves. But thirdly, and perhaps most importantly for the purposes of this book, abortion has wider-reaching repercussions for all of us, both as individuals and as a society.

For instance, the high number of abortions means that the national reproductive rate overall has now fallen to 1.65%, well below the 2.1% replacement level needed to keep the population size constant in the absence of migration.[4] In practical terms, this means that there will be lower numbers of people available to work, and increased pressure on our already over-strained resources to look after the elderly and infirm, as society becomes *top heavy*, with a steadily ageing population. Economically, the country will be forced to pay out ever more in pensions and health care, necessitating an increasingly heavy tax burden on the young, which many will resent. At the same time, it will mean that young people wanting to establish a home and family of their own will find it harder to buy a house and provide for their family. And even if mothers want to stay at home in the early years of their child's life, they won't be able to, because – with a partner or not – they simply won't be able to manage financially. To compound the problem, we will become even more reliant on immigration and temporary overseas workers, in order to ensure that vital jobs are filled and society runs smoothly. And while many immigrants integrate well, others may bring extremism with them and be hostile to our values, thus exacerbating social fragmentation and instability, potentially further eroding our national and cultural identity.

At the moment, procuring or assisting in an abortion in England and Wales remains a criminal offence, subject to exceptions set out in the Abortion Act 1967. Abortion is permitted up to 24 weeks where two medical practitioners agree there is a risk, greater than if the pregnancy is terminated, to the mother's physical or mental health, or to any existing children of her family. Beyond that, abortion is permitted up to term where there is risk of grave permanent injury to the physical or mental health of the pregnant woman; where there is a risk to her life, greater than if the pregnancy were terminated; or where there is substantial risk that the child, when born, would suffer from physical or mental abnormalities, such as to render him or her seriously handicapped. Currently this means, therefore, that women may seek abortion more or less on request up to 24 weeks, at which point the baby is judged capable of independent existence outside the womb. Beyond that date there needs to be a more clearly defined medical cause.

In Northern Ireland the situation is rather different. Until recently, abortion in the Province remained a criminal offence, with termination permitted only where a woman's life was at risk, or there was a danger of permanent and serious damage to her physical or mental health. However, all this changed in October 2019, when abortion was not just legalised, but completely decriminalised, following a vote by MPs at Westminster under the Northern Ireland (Executive Formation etc) Act, transferring control of the Province to Westminster, after failure to re-establish the Northern Irish Assembly at Stormont. Previously,

Labour MPs Stella Creasy and Conor McGinn had tabled amendments to the Bill extending access to abortion and same-sex marriage to the Province, to bring it into line with the rest of the UK. As result of the vote, s.58 of the Offences Against the Person Act 1861 was repealed for Northern Ireland, totally removing all prohibition against abortion, and giving Northern Ireland technically the most liberal abortion law in Europe. The situation now is that, under new law that came into force in March 2020, abortion on request and without condition is permitted up to 12 weeks, and thereafter is permitted up to 24 weeks where there is risk of injury to the woman's physical or mental health. There is no time limit for cases of fatal foetal abnormality.

However, notwithstanding the ease with which women in England, Wales, and now Northern Ireland, can access abortion, pressure to liberalise and yet further extend existing law has been growing, with pro-abortion activists in Parliament calling for complete decriminalisation up to birth. To put it another way, they argue that abortion - which is all about 'choice' and women's rights - should be 'medicalised', so that it is no longer subject to law at all, but becomes a routine procedure, on a par with tonsillectomy or breast enlargement.

In tribute to the millions of lives that have been lost, this book is about the hidden cost of abortion and the harm it does to society.

The first chapter, written by myself, looks at the history and evolution of abortion up to the present day, and examines the agenda behind current calls for reform. In particular, it looks at the involvement of 'big business', with its ever-increasing and insatiable drive for profit, which over the last decades has made abortion an aptly named industry. The drive behind population control is also examined, along with the effect of Kinsey's erroneous and pernicious insistence that we are all sexual animals from birth and that, therefore, sex is an inalienable human right – also from birth. The main thrust, however, remains the wider consequences flowing from abortion, with their damaging effects on society, culminating in the argument that we are killing off the human race.

In Chapter 2, *Medical Perspectives on Abortion*, Professor John Wyatt, Emeritus Professor of Neonatal Paediatrics at University College London, sets out the techniques used in medical and surgical abortions. He also provides an overview of foetal development, and describes ground-breaking medical advances which mean, routinely, that premature babies of 22 and 23 weeks can now not just survive, but thrive. If nothing else, he says, this means that the current time limit of 24 weeks for abortion is very out of date. He also raises the important issues of foetal pain and the response to stimuli, making the point that the unborn child is very far from being the passive and unconscious occupant of the mother's womb, as once thought, but, rather, is a vulnerable being responding to stimuli from a few weeks old, and capable of feeling severe pain. He argues, in sum, that there are strong and well-validated reasons not just for *not* extending the time limit for abortion, but for reducing it significantly, to take account of our improved understanding of foetal development and the lower age for survival.

Developing this theme, Robert S. Harris addresses the question of abortion and disability. Currently, as indicated above, abortion is not just permitted but often is actively encouraged where there is evidence of foetal abnormality. Such abnormalities may be relatively minor, such as the indication of a cleft palate, but may also, of course, extend to more severe and sometimes life-threatening impairment. Robert S. Harris argues that recommending abortion of the disabled is a form of eugenics, and a rejection and abuse of the right to life of the child, whose quality of life, once born, it is actually impossible to assess. Looking at the debates culminating in the passing of the Abortion Act, he shines a spotlight on the intricate, and still unresolved, problems of interpretation, especially as applied to the authorisation of abortion for disability. He shows how this has led to an abuse of the law's provisions. Examining what international law says about protecting the right to life of the unborn child with disability, he also points out that disability is one of the nine characteristics protected under the Equality Act 2010. He argues that our attitude towards a disabled child prior to birth, however, makes a mockery of such protection, while being judgmental and at odds with the supposed tolerance of our society. Rather than simply recommending abortion to parents, when they are told their unborn child will be physically or mentally impaired, he argues that, as a matter of justice, we should refrain from value judgments that simply assume such a child will have no worthwhile 'quality of life', and instead offer parents better information and more practical support to care for their disabled child.

Providing a theological perspective, Bishop Michael Nazir-Ali examines what the Bible says about the gift of life and when it starts. Citing many biblical references indicating that human life begins prior to birth, he looks in particular at the birth narratives of Jesus and John the Baptist, concluding that there is incontrovertible evidence that, for all humanity, God begins His work in and for us in the womb. Historically, he says, the Church has regarded abortion as unimaginable and prohibited by God's laws and purposes. But, acknowledging that society today takes a different stance, he goes on to look at the thorny question of 'ensoulment', examining the ethical and moral issues surrounding society's arbitrary imposition of a developmental time line, used to determine when termination may or may not be permissible. He also relates this to the more 'invisible' destruction of the embryo in procedures like dominant forms of IVF, medical experimentation and genetic diagnosis of disposition to disease.

The latter part of the book comes at the issue from a rather different perspective. In recent years much has been made in the press about the alleged activities of pro-life groups outside abortion clinics. It has been alleged that they harass, intimidate, and generally cause distress to women, and there have been attempts to impose exclusion or 'buffer' zones around clinics, preventing access. For example, in 2018 an exclusion order was made in Ealing, west London, stopping protestors from coming within 100 metres of the local Marie Stopes abortion clinic, while the following year a similar order was made for the Richmond clinic in south west London. Legal challenge failed to have the orders lifted, but the then Home Secretary, Sajid Javid, subsequently ordered all such zones to be removed, saying they were a disproportionate response.[5] Since that time, however, there have been renewed calls for the imposition of zones as the only way to stop protests getting worse,[6] and Ealing MP Dr Rupa Huq has, at the time of writing, a Private Member's bill before Parliament calling for the creation of 150 metre buffer zones around all clinics.[7]

Despite allegations of intimidation and harassment, however, in general pro-life campaigners are noted for being respectful, compassionate, and non-confrontational. But it cannot be denied that they are proving to be increasingly successful in providing the public with clear information as to what is actually involved in abortion, and it is without doubt that many distressed women, faced with an unplanned pregnancy, have been helped. The lives of many unborn babies have, as result, been saved. The final two chapters, therefore, look at the thinking and the activities of two such organisations.

In *Abortion – a Winnable Battle*, Andrew Stephenson, CEO and Founder of CBR UK (the Centre for Bioethical Reform, UK), takes the position that unevidenced assertions about 'morality' – i.e. simply saying that terminating the life of the unborn is wrong – have historically achieved nothing, because they have not given people any idea as to why it is wrong. Analysing past movements for social reform, he argues that successful campaigns – as, for example, with slavery – have always hinged on making injustice *visible*, so that it becomes a reality that cannot be simply glossed over or ignored. It is for this reason, he says, that CBR UK took the decision to display large banners showing the victims of abortion. Making the point that to change public policy we have first to change public opinion, he stresses that showing people the bloody reality of a dismembered baby brings home the reality of what is involved. His arguments, though disturbing, are compelling. Abortion is not simply the removal of a minor problem; it is the killing of another human being. If people are going unthinkingly to support 'social' abortion, they need to know what is involved, what it means.

Finally, in *Crisis Pregnancy – Offering Real Choice*, Clare McCullough of The Good Counsel Network, a group offering help and practical support to women seeking abortion, explains how distressed and vulnerable women, faced with the problem of unplanned pregnancy, will often change their minds about abortion when given practical and financial help, combined with companionship. The position the organisation takes, she emphasises, is never judgmental, but simply an unreserved offer to stand with women who have nowhere else to go and need help, if they are to keep their baby. And interspersed throughout the book are five testimonies from once-desperate women, who have received such help and are now proud mothers.

It has been both a joy and a privilege, for all of us involved, to put together this book, and to meet those working so tirelessly and valiantly to defend the right to life of the unborn. I extend my heartfelt thanks to the Voice for Justice UK team, and especially Robert S. Harris, who has worked so hard.

In putting together this book, we are aware that those advocating decriminalisation will oppose us vehemently. But it is our hope that, by demonstrating the full humanity of the unborn child, and pointing to his or her capacity to survive from as early as 21 weeks, we will have helped readers to recognise that the current time limit of 24 weeks is no longer appropriate. It urgently needs to be reduced. We would remind readers that prior to 1990 the time limit for abortion, based on the perceived age of viability, was 28 weeks. However, at that time the limit was reduced to 24 weeks, to take account of the advances in medical science that meant babies were routinely surviving at a lower gestational age. That is, Parliament realigned the law to correspond with medical advance. Medical science has now advanced yet further, and we urge that the law should catch up. As a practical first step, therefore, we urge a limit of 18 weeks – which would allow for improved future medical practice lowering the age of survival still further. But, as a matter of urgency, we also ask lawmakers to take account of the future economic and cultural welfare of our nation, which has been so disastrously impacted by current policy and practice in the area of abortion. The next generation, it seems, is being viewed as a disposable asset. It is no exaggeration to say that at this point in time, with population replacement rates across the developed world in serious decline, humanity stands at a crossroads. Unless, therefore, we take urgent measures to reverse the trend, the future, not just of our society, but of the whole of mankind, is in jeopardy.

Endnotes

[1] https://api.parliament.uk/historic-hansard/commons/1966/jul/22/medical-termination-of-pregnancy-bill (Accessed 18-11-20).

INTRODUCTION

2 https://www.gov.uk/government/publications/abortion-statistics-during-the-coronavirus-pandemic-january-to-june-2020/abortion-statistics-for-england-and-wales-during-the-covid-19-pandemic (Accessed 20-11-20).

3 https://www.ons.gov.uk/peoplepopulationandcommunity/birthsdeathsandmarriages/conceptionandfertilityrates/bulletins/conceptionstatistics/2018 (Accessed 20-11-20).

4 https://www.ons.gov.uk/peoplepopulationandcommunity/birthsdeathsandmarriages/livebirths/bulletins/birthsummarytablesenglandandwales/2019 (Accessed 19-11-20).

5 https://www.bbc.co.uk/news/uk-45509202 (Accessed 20-11-20).

6 https://www.stylist.co.uk/opinion/sajid-javid-abortion-clinic-buffer-zones-ruling-2018/226939 (Accessed 16-11-20).

7 https://publications.parliament.uk/pa/bills/cbill/58-01/0145/200186.pdf (Accessed 20-11-20).

Chapter One

THE INSANITY OF ABORTION – KILLING OFF THE HUMAN RACE

The Revd Lynda Rose

According to figures released by the Office for National Statistics on 13 June 2019,[1] in 2018 there was an overall total of 205,295 abortions performed on women in England and Wales. For women resident in those countries, the total was 200,605 – which made these figures the highest number since records began in 1974, and marked a 4% increase on 2017. Despite the rhetoric of the abortion lobby, therefore, increased and earlier access to contraceptive provision has not meant a decrease in the numbers of women seeking abortion, as had been argued by proponents for legalisation in 1967, but the reverse.

Roughly translated, the figures mean that under the terms of the Abortion Act 1967, around 4,000 unborn children are legally killed in the UK each week, which further translates into 530 terminations every 24 hours, or 22 every hour. Perhaps even more shockingly, since the Act was passed the British Isles has seen in total over 9,500,000 abortions. To put this in some kind of perspective, our population currently stands at around 66 million, meaning that in the last century we have legally killed around the equivalent of 14% of the population. To put it another way, the number of abortions carried out in the UK since 1967 would be equal to killing the entire population of Austria, or of Ireland and Singapore combined.

Some more figures: in 2018 there were 657,076 live births recorded in England and Wales.[2] Set against the 200,605 recorded abortions, this means that roughly one in four pregnancies ended in termination. In order for the population of a country to survive, replacement level fertility requires an average of 2.1 children per woman. The current fertility rate for the UK stands at 1.7 births per woman,[3] and it is falling. Over the next fifty or so years our population will almost certainly grow – but this will be as result of immigration, while the indigenous – ageing – British population moves towards extinction. However it is viewed, this will mark a major demographic shift, bringing in its wake possibly unsustainable cultural, political and economic challenge.

As a result of the damaging effects of birth control policies, this same situation is being replicated worldwide. Up until 2013, for example, China had a rigorously imposed one-child policy. As result, by 2016 the fertility rate had dropped to 1.6 births per woman. Even worse, the practice of sex-selective abortion by couples who wanted their only child to be a boy had led to a serious decline in the number of girls. In fact, by 2016 there was an estimated surplus of 30 million males, whose future prospects of marriage were inevitably seriously diminished, leading to fears of civil unrest and violence from young men with too much testosterone and no outlet for their pent-up energy. So at this point China took steps to remedy the decline, encouraging all couples to have at least two children. The question is, however, have they left it too late? Despite their best efforts, it rapidly became clear that many women, who up till then had been encouraged to focus on their careers, favoured economic security over the increased burden of more children, and were unwilling to comply. So much so that in some provinces the fertility rate has reportedly fallen to 0.89%, and the forecast is that by 2050 a third of the country's population will be made up of people over 60, putting severe strain on state services,[4] and on 'only' children struggling to care for increasing numbers of elderly relatives.[5]

In Russia too, where abortion has long been the main method of birth control, the falling birth rate has been and is a major cause of concern, with projections that by 2050 the population will have declined from 143 million to 111 million. The problem is seen as so acute that, as long ago as 2006, President Vladimir Putin called for incentives to encourage couples to have a second child.[6]

Notwithstanding such well-evidenced concerns for national depopulation and demographic destabilisation, however, abortion activists in the UK are today calling for the decriminalisation of abortion up to term, arguing that it should be treated simply as a woman's health care procedure attaching to her reproductive rights, and governed by medical regulatory frameworks. In the words of Professor Helen Stokes-Lampard, former chairwoman of the Royal College of GPs, "Ultimately, this is about providing non-judgmental care to our patients so that women who face the difficult decision to proceed with an abortion are not disadvantaged by the legal system."[7]

To put this argument another way, a woman's right to choose what happens to her own body overrides any putative 'right' on the part of her unborn child to life, so that the morality of such a decision becomes irrelevant. On this line of reasoning every effort must be made to minimise the inconvenient truth that abortion – presented as a fundamental human right for the woman - takes the life of another human being. This fiction – that the unborn child doesn't become a human being until birth – can only be sustained if no criminal sanctions attach. But given the fact that the UK already has, in effect, abortion on demand up to 24 weeks, the call for extension still seems hard to justify: exactly how are women's so-called reproductive rights upheld by the unquestioned right to kill an unborn child up to, and even including, the moment of birth? Surely, if a woman doesn't want her unborn child, the decision will have been made far earlier, so why does the right of termination have to continue up till the moment of birth?

To attempt to answer this question, we need to understand more about the background to abortion – specifically what motivated early advocates for legalisation, and the controlling powers behind similar campaigns today.

The situation before 1967

Prior to 1967, abortion in the UK was regulated by the Offences against the Person Act 1861, which made it an offence unlawfully to administer any poison or noxious thing, or to use any instrument, with the intention of procuring a miscarriage.[8] This applied both to a woman trying to abort her own child, and to anyone trying to help her, and the penalty was penal servitude for life or for a period not less than three years.[9]

Somewhat unhelpfully, the definition of what would be considered lawful was not spelt out, but the Bourne Case in 1938 subsequently ruled that a doctor might *lawfully* carry out an abortion where there were reasonable grounds for belief that the continuation of pregnancy would leave the mother a physical or mental wreck.[10] Even before 1967, therefore, an abortion could be performed on the NHS where there were serious and substantiated concerns for the mother's health.

Not many doctors, however, would agree to this, so that the majority of women wanting to rid themselves of an unwanted pregnancy were left with three options. First, they could attempt to self-induce a miscarriage, attempting to dislodge the foetus with a knitting needle, crochet hook, or the like. Or they could try taking herbs known to cause miscarriage, or drinking something like bleach, or – less toxically – gin, followed by a hot bath, giving a whole new meaning to 'mother's ruin'. Second, they could seek the help of a so-called back-street abortionist. This blanket term, however, requires some clarification, because not all were the evil and unskilled charlatans claimed. Some were undoubtedly enthusiastic amateurs, known locally as offering this kind of service, and who would 'help' for a small fee. Others, perhaps equally dangerous, might have had some rudimentary nursing experience, or have worked in a hospital – but still others would have been highly skilled doctors or nurses, offering the service either from compassion, or for a bit of non-taxable cash on the side. Third and last, if a woman had greater financial resources, she could overcome a doctor's scruples by paying him to sign the necessary certificates allowing her to have the operation carried out 'legally' in hospital. This, however, required serious money and was beyond the reach of most women, so that by far the greatest number went for option 2.

Advocates for abortion have long maintained that the highest cause of maternal death prior to 1967 was injury sustained at the hands of unqualified women, carrying out sometimes horrific procedures – but is this true? There were, without question, casualties. And, reportedly, some A&E departments even took on extra staff on Fridays (pay day) to deal with the influx of women suffering the after-effects of a botched abortion.[11] But it is equally beyond question that the claims have been greatly exaggerated. The uncharitable might even say they have been deliberately distorted.

Background

When the Liberal MP David Steel proposed his abortion Bill in 1966, he claimed there were between 40,000 to 100,000 illegal abortions a year.[12] It is, however, impossible to verify these figures. For a start, the yearly numbers recorded as abortion included miscarriage, which rather distorted analysis at the outset. A lot of pregnancies end in miscarriage, even today – but in the case of illegal abortion, a doctor was only ever called in where there were 'untoward symptoms'. In other words, doctors only got to know that something illegal had taken place when something went wrong. *Records of medical intervention where this happened are relatively sparce.*

Campaigners say that doctors falsified their records in order to protect women from prosecution, but in evidence given to the Birkett Inquiry into abortion in 1937, the Midwives Institute said that in their opinion the number of illegal abortions was low, and that most working class women, faced with unwanted pregnancy, simply went ahead and had the baby.[13] One would think, since these midwives were at the front line, that they would have had a clear idea of what they were talking about.

But, logically, this means that if the numbers cited by David Steel and his fellow activists were anywhere near as high as claimed, a very large number must have been highly successful – because there wasn't a problem, no doctor was called, and the women went on to have more children. This, however, seriously undermines the argument for abortion reform, so what was really going on?

A little bit of history

From earliest times there have always been women – and sometimes men – who regarded their unborn child as an inconvenience. The earliest recorded evidence of induced abortion dates back to 1550 BC, and is found in the Egyptian Ebers Papyrus,[14] but the practice was widely accepted in the Greco-Roman world. Indeed, in ancient Rome it was regarded as morally equivalent to infanticide, which was permitted up to around the age of two, when it was thought the child acquired some degree of 'personhood' and therefore protectable rights.[15] Other cultures had similar acceptance of a woman's right to get rid of her baby. But what this all meant was that from earliest times different cultures developed their own abortion techniques and procedures, ranging from the use of natural abortifacients, such as herbs, to the development of specially designed sharpened instruments for the extraction of the foetus, a job usually undertaken by midwives.

But as with all medical practice, before the advent of penicillin and improved hygiene, casualty rates for the women concerned were high. Many died, especially where some kind of instrument was involved to try and procure miscarriage – perforation of the womb was very likely. But it is worth pointing out that, in times gone by, similar outcomes followed on from any treatments involving open wounds or surgery. So fast-forward to the early twentieth century, and the claimed high mortality rates resulting from back-street abortions are hardly surprising. One might even say they were to be expected! What advocates for reform did not mention, however, were the similar high mortality rates that followed 'legal' abortions carried out in hospital. As pointed out by Dr Peter Saunders in his excellent short article, *How many women really died from abortions prior to the Abortion Act?,* survival rates, whether in hospital or in someone's back room, were directly correlated to standards of hygiene and infection control. Once medical care improved, the high levels of maternal mortality from all causes began to fall dramatically.[16] But this had started to become evident, as he points out, long before abortion was legalised.

It was perhaps, therefore, disingenuous to put forward as the main argument for reform the fact that so many women were dying as the result of 'back-street' abortion. Without doubt, as noted above, there were casualties, but 'legalising' abortion for all was very far from being the gold-standard solution that it was represented to be by advocates for reform. Similarly, exploitation of the tragedy caused by thalidomide to call for legalisation of abortion for disability was fundamentally dishonest, because this was essentially a case of pharmaceutical malpractice, indicating a need for tighter regulation.

For those unfamiliar with the details of this scandal, in the early 1960s thalidomide was marketed as a safe drug to combat morning sickness. It was, however, very far from safe, and led to high numbers of children being born severely deformed. It was subsequently withdrawn from use in the UK in 1961, after an Australian doctor, William McBride, wrote a letter to the Lancet connecting the deformities with the drug.[17] Aborting affected babies was not, and never could have been, the answer to the problem, but that didn't stop activists from exploiting the tragedy, arguing that it would be kinder for such babies if they were never born.

What then was the real agenda driving so-called reform?

To understand the driving force behind calls for abortion reform in the early part of the twentieth century, it is necessary to go back a couple of hundred years to the eighteenth century, which had seen the emergence of a growing belief in human progress. Enlightenment thinkers such as Turgot[18] and Condorcet[19] believed that humanity would continue to evolve, leading over time to the development of a utopian society. However, this view was challenged in1798 by an English clergyman, Thomas Malthus, who rose to prominence after publication of his controversial book, *An Essay on the Principle of Population.*[20]

Malthus argued that whenever social conditions improved there was a corresponding growth in the population. He believed, however, that global resources, including mankind's capacity for the production of food, remained finite, so that any rise in population would inevitably be followed by decline. It would also, and most importantly, operate to prevent social progress. And so, in order to avoid famine, disease, and war, resulting from the inevitable increased competition for limited resources, Malthus argued that the numbers of the poor (who, in his view, contributed little of value to society and were a drain) needed to be regulated. To aid the economy and ensure the future wellbeing of society, he therefore advocated population control, aimed in particular at limiting the birth rate of the impoverished.

Perhaps unsurprisingly, his ideas did not gain widespread acceptance.

Indeed, they were rejected by Capitalists and Marxists alike – the former because they felt it was their duty to help improve the conditions of the poor, and the latter because they believed it was the efforts of the 'exploited' poor that led to the production of wealth, which should be used for the common good. But notwithstanding the affront to both middle class and revolutionary sensibilities, in the nineteenth century Malthus' views managed to inspire a handful of radicals.

First, there was the group led by Charles Bradlaugh, founder in 1866 of the National Secular Society,[21] aided by his close associate Annie Besant.[22] Supporters of the pair rejected belief in God and regarded the poor as a burden on the wealthy, who, they argued, were by definition more highly evolved – poverty being proof of inferiority. Strongly influenced by Darwin – himself influenced by Malthus – this group argued that the improvement of the human race could only be achieved by promoting the survival of the fittest (by definition, the wealthy and prosperous), and discouraging reproduction by those of lower evolutionary status. To achieve this they advocated the use of contraception.

They were quickly followed by a second group, known as Eugenicists, who wanted to improve the genetic quality of the population by not just discouraging, but actually *preventing* reproduction of the 'inferior' - whom they identified as the physically and mentally unfit, and the generational poor, labelling them 'undesirables'. According to their way of thinking, the strengthening of the gene pool could never be achieved by reliance on contraception – which at best was hit-or-miss. So they argued instead that only the physically and mentally fit should be allowed to marry and have children, with union between those deemed inferior not just discouraged, but actively disallowed. To further their ends, they advocated segregation, birth control, sterilisation, abortion, euthanasia, and extermination ... which was exactly, of course, what emerged in Nazi Germany and led to ethnic cleansing.

Over time these two groups merged, but the underlying motive for both was a belief in the perfectibility of the human race by the eradication of the unfit, the degenerate, and the poor, who were seen as a drain on society.

In 1936 the Abortion Law Reform Association (ARLA) was established to campaign specifically for the legalisation of abortion. Of its four founder members, Dr Joan Malleson, Stella Browne and Alice Jenkins, were all members of the Eugenics Society, while the fourth, Janet Chance, was a Malthusian. Their shared vision, of course, was the improvement of the human race, by discouraging reproduction amongst the 'undesirables'.

The same is true of Marie Stopes, the UK's early pioneer of birth control and abortion. The organisation, which bears her name, is still one of the largest abortion providers internationally, and the second largest – with over sixty clinics – here in England.[23] It is entirely true that the family planning clinics run by Ms Stopes – she never adopted her married name, Roe – were always clustered in deprived areas, but she was far from being the altruistic campaigner for women's rights and the champion of the downtrodden poor, presented by the women's movement today. Rather, her expressed aim was to stop the unfit from breeding, and she even lobbied Parliament to pass laws to make sterilisation compulsory, in order to "… ensure the sterility of the hopelessly rotten and radically diseased … by the elimination of wasteful lives."[24]

Her objective, therefore, was to prevent the propagation of "the inferior, the depraved, and the feeble-minded." Nor did she like people who were "half-caste", stating in 1934 that they too should be sterilised at birth.[25] It is perhaps no surprise to discover that she idolised Hitler – so much so that she sent him love letters and a bound copy of her poems.

This then is the background to abortion: so-called reform was driven not by a desire to empower women and gain respect for their "sexual rights", but rather by the desire to eliminate the inferior, the feeble-minded, and the poor.

The agenda behind "reform" today

Today, whatever ostensible arguments are put forward by campaigners, abortion liberalisation is still not, in reality, about women's rights; instead it is about money, big business, and population control. Over the last year especially, overpopulation has been presented as one of the world's greatest environmental challenges. Unless we take action fast, pundits warn, we face catastrophic degradation, not just to the quality and length of human life, but to humanity's continued existence. Natural resources are seriously depleted, they argue; there's not enough food, and sustainable drinking water is running out, so that people will starve, and we'll see an increase in disease. The only possible solution is that all of us should have fewer children![26] All this is remarkably similar to the arguments put forward by Malthus.

Counterpointed against this, however, is the ever-increasing Western insistence that the immediate gratification of sexual desire, unrestrained by considerations of morality, is an inalienable human right. This view has its origins in the work of people such as Alfred Kinsey, the American zoologist specializing in gall wasps, who became a self-proclaimed world authority on sex, after founding the Kinsey Institute for Research into Sex, Gender and Reproduction at Indiana University in 1947. His work, looking into and celebrating sexual gratification, revolutionized the American approach to sexual ethics. More significantly, he rejected heterosexual norms, arguing that traditional morality was based on superstition, and that men and women are at heart sexual beings, who should not be judged by erroneous "socially pretended custom". For Kinsey, indeed, any idea of sexual restraint flew in the face of biological reality, a view that extended even to children.

Much of Kinsey's work has in recent years been discredited – a large part of his research, for example, was based on work with known sex offenders, including male prostitutes and child molesters, rendering his so-called findings highly questionable. But, even so, his influence has persisted. In his controversial book, *Sexual Behavior in the Human Male*,[27] for instance, he claimed that 46% of male subjects in the course of their adult life reacted sexually to persons of both sexes, and that 37% had had at least one homosexual experience. He also detailed experiments recording juvenile experience of orgasm over periods ranging from 1 to 24 hours, the youngest juvenile involving a baby of 5 months, who, as the result of manual stimulation

24

by the researcher, reportedly experienced three orgasms (time period unspecified).[28] From this, Kinsey concluded that the sexual impulse cannot and should not be artificially restrained by social constraint, and that children are sexual beings from birth. It is indeed this view that underpins the delivery of so-called non-judgmental sex education to children in schools today, fuelling expectation that they will have sex from early adolescence.

We therefore have a dilemma: the unquestioned right of all of us to have sex whenever and wherever we choose, combined with the "moral" imperative not to reproduce. So how do we resolve this? Simple. Society promotes the use of contraception from age 11 and, where that fails, it provides abortion. Which, of course, is where big business and money come in.

It is estimated that by 2022 the global contraceptive market will generate revenue of $43,812 million.[29] Abortion is similarly lucrative. For example, in its financial returns for 2018, lodged on 29 May 2019, Marie Stopes International, subsequently renamed MSI Reproductive Choices, reported a total income of £296.8 million.[30] Reportedly, both BPAS (British Pregnancy Advisory Service) and MSI Reproductive Choices want to increase the proportion of abortions in the UK, with Anne Furedi, former Chief Executive of BPAS, calling abortion just another form of birth control and a woman's right. She has in fact repeatedly called for the removal of all restrictions[31] and, in the run up to the 2019 General Election, launched a campaign to get candidates to pledge support for the total decriminalisation of abortion – on demand, for any reason, and up to birth. In launching the campaign, she said, "I want to be very, very clear and blunt … there should be no legal upper limit."[32]

Fearless freedom fighter for the erroneously named weaker sex? Or callous exploiter of deluded and vulnerable women?

Unpalatable as it may appear, the drive to liberalise abortion law is not at heart about helping downtrodden women and furthering the cause of equality. It is about profit – and the logic is blindingly simple. The more sex people have, the more they will need family planning. The more contraception fails, the more women will need abortion. And if, on top of that, abortion providers can push the line that in order to save the planet men and women have a social responsibility to have fewer children – while reinforcing the line that sex is a natural urge that shouldn't be restrained – then that too is all to the good, because it will increase business.

However it is dressed up, this is a serious distortion of reality. The truth is that for the last seventy years women have been the victims of a global con trick – it is still going on – and because of it humanity as a whole is facing disaster. We are literally killing off the human race.

Some inconvenient truths

Wherever in the world there is mass provision of contraception, with abortion being hailed as a female right, we are witnessing an alarming decline in fertility, with catastrophic results for the population. In fact, the only countries where such decline is not happening, and where there are still high fertility rates, are those that are classified as poor and underdeveloped. Niger, for example, has a reproductive rate of 7.153; Somalia 6.123; Angola 5.589; Uganda 5.546.[33] And it is these countries, under the guise of human rights, that are now being subjected to major reform programmes by the UN, aimed at defending women's so-called reproductive rights and giving them a better life.[34]

By contrast, very little is being done to help countries at the other end of the scale to strengthen the family and encourage couples to have more children. And yet, if we want to avoid cultural and social disintegration, coupled with economic decline, this is what is needed. Increased access to birth control and abortion does not empower women, nor does it help gender equality. On the contrary, it can only facilitate male sexual exploitation, by encouraging promiscuity and removing all need for commitment. This will not, and cannot, alleviate poverty in Africa. In fact, it can only make women there more vulnerable, because it will inevitably further weaken marriage and the family, as it has already done here in the West, leaving growing numbers of single mothers to fend for themselves and bring up their children without help.

The situation in the UK

But the UK is not an underdeveloped, financially challenged country like those in sub-Saharan Africa, of course, and the situation is very different. So maybe the legalisation of abortion on demand and up to birth might actually help! Maybe decriminalising abortion really would empower women, freeing them from sexual slavery and financial dependence on men. And maybe, given the overcrowding of our country as the result of immigration, restricting the birth rate is the socially responsible thing to do.

These arguments are both erroneous and misleading. As already pointed out, where there is a risk of injury to the physical or mental health of the pregnant woman, or where there is substantial risk of serious physical or mental injury to the unborn child,[35] abortion is permitted in England, Scotland and Wales up to 24 weeks which, until recently, was the age at which it was thought a child could survive, independent of its mother, outside the womb. For all practical purposes, therefore, this is 'abortion on demand' up to 24 weeks, and it is difficult to see how the cause of 'gender equality' can be advanced by extending the legal right to kill a child up to 40+ weeks, when any decision to terminate would surely have been taken far earlier. These days, when we protest against boiling live lobsters and breeding animals for food, the argument seems wantonly cruel.

Similarly, given that the country's birth rate is already well below replacement level for maintenance of the indigenous population, why logically should we compound the problem by further discouraging women from having babies? A more sensible approach would surely be to cap immigration to sustainable levels, and encourage couples to have more children, supported by fiscal and tax benefits.

The inescapable conclusion is that abortion reform, however it is dressed up, is not about women's rights at all, but rather about profits for the abortion industry and controlling the global population, culling the vulnerable and disadvantaged so as to allow the dwindling numbers of those left to maintain their lifestyle, free of the burden of having to provide for those who cannot provide for themselves.

It is surely time for this hypocrisy to end, and for the right to life of the unborn to be upheld.

Endnotes

---

[1] https://assets.publishing.service.gov.uk/government/uploads/system/uploads/attachment_data/file/808556/Abortion_Statistics_England_and_Wales_2018_1_.pdf

[2] https://www.ons.gov.uk/peoplepopulationandcommunity/birthsdeathsandmarriages/livebirths/datasets/birthsummarytables

[3] https://www.ons.gov.uk/peoplepopulationandcommunity/birthsdeathsandmarriage/livebirths/bulletins/birthsummarytablesenglandandwales/2017

[4] See the interesting article examining these issues in 2015 in *The Guardian*: https://www.theguardian.com/commentisfree/2015/nov/01/china-one-child-policy (Accessed 19-12-19).

[5] Ibid.

[6] "Many Russian women use abortion as their sole course of birth control, and an estimated 930,000 women terminate a pregnancy each year. Surveys indicate that 72% of the population wants abortion to stay legal." *Population Decline in Russia*, Matt Rosenberg, https://www.thoughtco.com/population-decline-in-russia-1435266 (Accessed 10-10-19).

[7] https://www.thetimes.co.uk/article/royal-college-of-gps-calls-for-abortion-to-be-decriminalised-stlrd9ngd (Accessed 10-12-19).

[8] "Every woman, being with child, who, with intent to procure her own miscarriage, shall unlawfully administer to herself any poison or other noxious thing, or shall unlawfully use any instrument or other means whatsoever with the like intent, and whosoever, with intent to procure the miscarriage of any woman, whether she be or be not with child, shall unlawfully administer to her or cause to be taken by her any poison or other noxious thing, or shall unlawfully use any instrument or other means whatsoever with the like intent, shall be guilty of felony, and being convicted thereof shall be liable . . . to be kept in penal servitude for life ..." Offences against the person Act 1861 (https://www.legislation.gov.uk/ukpga/Vict/24-25/100/section/58).

[9] Ibid.

[10] *R v Bourne* [1939] 1 K.B. 687. In this case a 14 year old girl was gang raped by five soldiers and became pregnant as a result. Alec Bourne, an eminent gynaecologist, was charged with performing an illegal abortion, but was acquitted because he argued that her mental state meant she could not have the child without suffering irreparable mental damage.

[11] See, for example, the views of the women's rights campaigner, Diane Munday, https://www.independent.co.uk/life-style/health-and-families/illegal-abortion-1960s-sixties-uk-pro-choice-activist-diane-munday-bpas-a7657726.html (Accessed 11-12-19).

[12] HC Deb 22 July 1966 vol 732 col 1071.

[13] See, Midwives' Institute, memorandum to the Birkett Enquiry [MH71-22AC Paper 37].

[14] See, https://web.archive.org/web/20030701162741/http://big.berkeley.edu/ifplp.history.pdf (Accessed 14-8-19).

[15] *Roman infanticide, modern abortion*, Roger Crisp. Practical Ethics, University of Oxford http://blog.practicalethics.ox.ac.uk/2010/07/roman-infanticide-modern-abortion/ (Accessed 14-8-19).

[16] *How many women really died from abortions prior to the Abortion Act?* Dr Peter Saunders, CMF blogs 12-06-190619, https://cmfblog.org.uk/2012/ 06/17/how-many-women-really-died-from-abortions-prior-to-the-abortion-act/

[17] See his obituary, *William McBride: alerted the world to the dangers of thalidomide in fetal development*, BMJ 6-8-18, https://www.bmj.com/content/362/bmj.k3415 (Accessed 15-8-19).

[18] Anne-Robert-Jacques Turgot (1727-81), a Minister to Louis XVI, who wrote two influential works, *A Philosophical Review of the Successive Advances of the Human Mind* and *On Universal History*.

[19] Marie Jean Caritat, Marquis de Condorcet (1743-1794), wrote *Outlines of an historical view of the Progress of the human mind*.

[20] *An essay on the principle of population, as it affects the future improvement of society. With remarks on the speculations of Mr. Godwin, M. Condorcet and other writers*. First published anonymously by J. Johnson, London, 1798. Author subsequently identified as Thomas Robert Malthus. https://archive.org/details/essayonprincipl00malt/page/n8 (Accessed 26-11-19).

[21] Charles Bradlaugh, political activist and well-known atheist. Subsequently became Liberal MP for Northampton.

[22] Annie Besant, Fabian, theosophist, women's rights activist, and writer. Of Irish extraction, she became one of the most prominent speakers for the National Secular Society, and the first woman actively to endorse contraception as a means of alleviating poverty.

[23] https://www.mariestopes.org.uk (Accessed 10-11-19).

[24] https://archive.org/details/radiantmotherhoo00stopuoft/page/222 (Accessed 19-11-19).

[25] http://www.mix-d.org/museum/timeline/marie-stopes-and-the-sterilisation-of-half-castes (Accessed 28-02-20).

[26] https://www.everythingconnects.org/overpopulation-effects.html (Accessed 10-8-19).

[27] Alfred C. Kinsey, Wardell R. Pomeroy, and Clyde E, Martin. Sexual Behavior in the Human Male. Philadelphia, Pa: W.B. Saunders: 1948 ISBN 978-0-253-33412-1.

[28] The table from the book, showing the number and frequency of orgasms in pre-adolescent males, is reproduced by Judith Reisman, http://www.drjudithreisman.com/archives/2010/10/table_34.html (Accessed 8-10-19).

[29] https://www.alliedmarketresearch.com/contraceptives-market (Accessed 19-11-19).

[30] https://www.mariestopes.org/resources/financial-statement-and-annual-report-2018/ (Accessed 19-11-19).

[31] https://www.dailymail.co.uk/news/article-4673346/Abortion-no-form-birth-control.html (Accessed 19-11-19).

[32] See, https://righttolife.org.uk/news/uks-largest-abortion-provider-asking-mp-candidates-to-pledge-to-introduce-abortion-up-to-birth/ (Accessed 26-11-19).

[33] http://worldpopulationreview.com/countries/total-fertility-rate/ (Accessed 8-10-19).

[34] See, for example, the report: *Women's empowerment and reproductive health* https://www.unfpa.org/sites/default/files/pubpdf/women_empowerment_eng.pdf; or *Reproductive Rights and Human Rights: A handbook for national human rights institutions*, published by the United Nations Population Fund, the Danish Institute for Human Rights, and the Office of the High Commissioner for Human Rights 2014, https://www.ohchr.org/Documents/Publications/NHRIHandbook.pdf (Both accessed 10-11-19).

[35] See, https://www.mariestopes.org.uk/abortion-services/abortion-and-your-rights/ (Accessed 9-12-19).

Lucy's Story

When I discovered I was pregnant, I made an appointment with my GP.

During this time, our financial situation wasn't good. My husband and I were in the UK on visas. I was here on a student visa and I was not allowed to work. Due to visa issues, neither was my husband allowed to work for a while, so it was difficult. I was living in one room with my husband and eight-year old daughter. We had very little space. We thought that having another child would be a great strain on us financially. It seemed that the only option was a termination.

I told the doctor that because of financial difficulties, I wanted an abortion. He said okay. He gave me the telephone number of the Marie Stopes abortion clinic in Ealing, West London. When I went for my appointment, they did a scan and told me I was 19 weeks pregnant. But my reports were saying I was 16 weeks pregnant.

The person at the clinic said they first wanted to speak to my GP. They asked me to come back the next day. I cried the whole night before this second appointment. I really didn't want an abortion, but I thought I didn't have any choice.

When I returned to the clinic, as I entered the gate, Karen from the Good Counsel Network (GCN) approached me and offered a leaflet. She asked me if I needed any help. We spoke for a little while and she hugged me. I started crying. Karen told me I could visit their Women's Centre and have a chat with someone, if I wanted to.

She told me that I would be offered all the financial help I needed, if I decided to have my baby. After thinking about this offer, I felt I should drop it altogether, because I didn't know for sure that any real help would materialise from these people, whom I didn't know. I was in a foreign country and didn't know anyone. Would help really come from strangers? At first, I told the abortion clinic I needed more time to think about it.

I then agreed to visit the Women's Centre, where Clare, the woman in charge, gave me the phone numbers of a few mothers who were already receiving financial help to support their children. She said I could talk to them if I wished. If I didn't feel assured that help would be given, speaking to them might help. Clare explained that these women had been receiving help from the Women's Centre for a number of years.

I called a couple of mothers. They told me they had been receiving support for a few years. Speaking to them made me see my situation differently. I told Clare that if I had my child, we would need at least two bedrooms. I would sleep in one room with my husband and baby, while the other would be for my young daughter. She said my needs would be met and that I need not worry.

Clare also offered me the opportunity to have a scan. When I saw the baby, I literally started crying. I then felt that I couldn't have the abortion. I would regret it. It would be wrong. Actually, when you get the scan done at the abortion centre, they never show you the images. Only the doctors see them.

As we were also being offered new accommodation, I was now sure that I wanted to have my child. When I told the abortion clinic that I had made my mind up, and didn't want an abortion, they didn't talk any further about this. I don't think they care.

When our baby boy was born, we were provided with the accommodation that was promised. We paid what we could afford, and the people from GCN paid the outstanding amount. They also purchased a cot and a pushchair. They have continued to buy all the groceries we have needed as a family, as well as a regular supply of diapers.

Our son, whose name is Thomas, is now five years old. The people at GCN are continuing to support us, allowing us to buy clothes and shoes. They also help us with clothes for our older child. Since Thomas was born, my whole life has changed. He is now in Year One of school. Even my daughter has a better life now, because we are living in a nicer home. When I talk about all this, I get very emotional. I now feel my family is complete and it makes me happy.

When I hear that they are banning people offering help from standing outside abortion centres, I believe this is wrong. If a woman wants an abortion, she can have one. But if a woman doesn't want one because she is being offered help from people outside the clinics, why should this be stopped? Why should women be denied this help? It cannot be right. They are giving women a choice. How can that be wrong? The NHS doesn't give women these choices. And neither do abortion clinics – they are just making money from abortions!

Only recently, I was phoned by a woman who had an appointment scheduled for an abortion. Like me, she wanted to speak to a mother who had already received financial support. I told her about my experience. After hearing what I said, she decided she would keep her baby. Hearing this made me so happy. She changed her mind because she now knew of a real-life example.

Chapter Two

MEDICAL PERSPECTIVES ON ABORTION

John Wyatt

Emeritus Professor of Neonatal Paediatrics,
University College London

This chapter provides, first, up-to-date information on the techniques that are currently employed for surgical and medical abortions, and then a review of current scientific understanding concerning fetal development. Next it provides an overview of the survival and development of premature babies, and then addresses the scientific and clinical evidence about fetal sentience and the capacity of the fetus to experience pain at different stages of development.

A note on terminology

In medical terminology 'abortion' refers to the interruption of pregnancy in general. The term is used both for *spontaneous abortion* (which is described in lay parlance as a *miscarriage*), and for *induced abortion*, which is a medical procedure to cause interruption of the pregnancy. In the chapter that follows, the word 'abortion' is used to refer to *induced abortion*.

Pregnancies are normally dated from the time of the last menstrual period – this is described as the gestational age. Fertilisation of the mother's egg by the sperm normally occurs approximately 2 weeks after the last period. Hence an embryo that has a gestational age of 6 weeks is actually 4 weeks from fertilisation. This is frequently a source of confusion in the literature, and it is important to be precise as to whether gestational age or post-conceptual (post-fertilisation) age is being referred to.

The fertilised egg is described as an embryo from the point of fertilisation until the end of the 8th week after the date of the last period, or 6 weeks from fertilisation. Following 8 weeks the developing human is described as a fetus.[1]

1. ABORTION METHODS

Abortion methods are divided into surgical and medical techniques.

Surgical abortion

Before the procedure an ultrasound of the womb is obtained. This confirms the presence of a viable embryo or fetus and allows the gestational age to be assessed.

Surgical abortions are divided into i) vacuum aspiration, and ii) dilatation and evacuation.

i) Vacuum aspiration can be carried out up to about 15 weeks gestational age. It involves dilatation of the neck of the womb (the cervix) and the passage of a suction catheter through the cervix into the womb. The tissue of the embryo or fetus, together with the placenta and supporting structures, is then destroyed and removed. Vacuum aspiration can be carried out under a local or general anaesthetic.

ii) Dilatation and evacuation is carried out between 15 and 23 weeks and 6 days gestational age. It involves dilatation of the cervix followed by insertion of surgical forceps into the cavity of the womb. The fetus is dismembered and removed in pieces through the cervix. A general anaesthetic is always given to the mother, but in standard surgical practice no specific pain relief is provided for the fetus.

Medical abortion

A medical abortion involves the administration of two separate medications. The first medication, mifepristone, works by blocking the actions of the natural hormone progesterone. Mifepristone leads to the breaking down of the lining of the womb, leading normally to the death of the embryo or fetus. The second medication, misoprostol, is taken after a period of 24-48 hours. This causes the womb to contract forcefully, leading to the expulsion of the embryo or fetus.

With medical abortion up to the 10 weeks gestational age, the first medication is usually taken in the abortion clinic or hospital and the second medication is taken at home. With medical abortion beyond 10 weeks, the second medication is given in the clinic or hospital. The British Pregnancy Advisory Service (BPAS) website has the following description: "On average it takes about 6 hours for the labour and delivery, but this can vary. In some cases it may be quicker, but in others it may take over 24 hours and you will need to stay overnight in the clinic. In a minority of procedures, the placenta does not pass spontaneously and it is necessary to perform an additional procedure, usually under general anaesthetic, to remove it."[2]

Medical abortions accounted for 71% of all abortions in England and Wales in 2018. The proportion of medical abortions has almost doubled in the last ten years from 37% in 2008. Medical abortion has been the most common method of abortion since 2014.[3]

Feticide

In medical abortion at later gestational ages there is the possibility that the fetus will be born alive. Since 1996 the Royal College of Obstetricians and Gynaecologist (RCOG) has advised that legal abortion must not be allowed to result in a live birth. Hence the RCOG stated that "in the later weeks of pregnancy, methods used during abortion to stop the fetal heart should be swift and should involve a minimum of injury to fetal tissue."[4]

Abortion beyond 22 weeks of gestation usually involves injection into the fetal heart of a lethal medication designed to cause cardiac arrest (usually potassium chloride, a chemical which causes cardiac arrest). Sometimes medication is injected into the amniotic fluid; in this case it can take several hours for the fetal heartbeat and fetal movements to stop.[5]

2. FETAL DEVELOPMENT

During monthly ovulation a single egg is secreted into the Fallopian tube. Fertilisation occurs within the Fallopian tube when a single sperm enters the egg, and the nuclear material from mother and father fuse together to create a unique embryonic human being. The process of the merging of the DNA from sperm and egg occurs over a few hours. Once the new human genome is created, cell division occurs, with the embryo growing from 1 to 8 cells over the first 4 days as it passes down the Fallopian tube. As the embryo continues to grow it is now called a 'blastocyst'. Implantation of the embryo into the wall of the womb usually occurs around 9 days after fertilisation (approximately 3 weeks of gestation).

At around 18 to 19 days after fertilisation, the heart begins to form. The heart is the first functional organ to develop, and it starts to beat and pump blood at around day 21 or 22. The brain and the spine are also forming. At this stage the embryo is about 5 mm in length and it is possible to identify the embryo and surrounding structures by an ultrasound scan.

By 7 weeks gestational age (5 weeks after fertilisation), the embryo is about 1 cm long. The hands, feet, mouth and face are all present. Movements of the embryo can be detected by ultrasound. By 10 weeks gestational age, all the body organs are present. The fetus can be observed to be yawning, stretching, and moving actively. Sensory receptors are present on the face and lips. The fetus responds to touch from this time onwards. Over the next few weeks touch receptors develop all over the body surface. Nerve connections between the skin and the spinal cord are present from about 10 weeks. The cerebral cortex (the lining surface of the brain) also starts to develop from about 10 weeks.

By 12 weeks gestation the fetus is sucking and swallowing, and showing 'rooting' behaviour, moving the mouth towards a hand or foot or other body part. A range of facial expressions can be seen by ultrasound from about 14 weeks onwards.

By 17 weeks cortical development is progressing and a critical region of brain cells, called the subplate zone, develops immediately below the cortex. Nerve connections from the body to the subplate zone are present from about 17 weeks onwards. An active biological stress response to damaging stimuli, such as the insertion of a needle, can be observed from 16 weeks onwards, and a rise in stress hormones can be detected from 18 weeks onwards.[6]

The fetus can be shown to have some response to sound from about 20 weeks of gestation. Preterm babies born from 22-23 weeks gestation onwards show evidence of pain perception by screwing up their faces and breath-holding in response to stimuli such as a heel-prick or needle insertion.[7] By 26 weeks the full anatomical system for pain sensation has been formed, and preterm babies of the same gestational age show a complex range of behaviours, accompanied by simultaneous changes in electrical activity in the cortex.[8] Fetuses show a characteristic alerting response to external noise and vibration from about 26 weeks onwards. Sleep-wake cycling can be seen in the fetus from 30 weeks onwards.

The brain is the last organ to develop. The basic anatomical structure of the brain is complete by 18 weeks of gestation, but there is rapid brain growth and continuing development of brain connections from this time onwards to full-term and beyond. The brain continues to make new connections over the first years of life, so there is a sense in which the process of brain development never stops.

3. SURVIVAL OF PREMATURE BABIES

There has been a steady improvement in the survival of premature babies over the last 60-70 years. A survey of the world literature on the outcome of very premature babies was published in the Lancet in 1981.[9]

The authors showed that in the period 1946-50 no babies born at less than 1000g weight (which is equivalent to being born at less than 28 weeks gestation) survived. In the period 1966-70, approximately 10-15% of babies born at less than 28 weeks gestation survived. This information was used, at the time when the 1967 Abortion Act was being framed, to establish 28 weeks gestation as the limit of viability.

The authors of the Lancet paper showed that, because of advances in medical care, by the period 1976-77 approximately 30% of babies born at less than 1000g (equivalent to below 28 weeks gestation) were surviving.

In 1990 a Europe-wide study on the survival of very premature babies was published in the Lancet.[10] This showed that survival had become common between 24 and 28 weeks of gestation. However, survival below 24 weeks was almost non-existent. When the Abortion Act was amended by Parliament in 1990, 24 weeks was taken as the gestational age at which viability commenced.

Since 1990 there have been continued improvements in the prospects for survival of extremely premature babies. In one study, based in a single neonatal intensive care unit in central London (University College London Hospitals, UCLH), which was published in the international scientific journal *Acta Paediatrica* in 2008,[11] survival at 22 and 23 weeks was zero in the period 1981-85, but this steadily improved to around 50% of babies born alive at this gestational age in the period 1996-2000.

Two large nationwide studies of survival around the limits of viability from hospitals across the UK were undertaken in 1995 and 2006, called EPICURE studies.[12] These showed that survival at 24 weeks gestation rose from approximately 35% in 1995 to approximately 45% in 2006. Survival at 23 weeks gestation rose from approximately 20% in 1995 to approximately 28% in 2006, and survival at 22 weeks gestation rose from approximately 5% to 15%.

These percentages represent average figures obtained across a large number of hospitals with differing facilities and expertise. The percentage of surviving babies is lower compared with the UCLH study which came from a single major centre. However, the overall take-home message is the same. Survival at 22 and 23 weeks has steadily improved since 1990 when the Abortion Act was amended. Because of continuing improvements in care it is likely that the survival prospects for premature babies born at the time of writing, 2019, will be significantly better than for those born in 2006 when the second EPICURE study was undertaken.[13]

The same phenomenon has been seen in many published studies from advanced healthcare systems around the world.[14,15] Survival at 22 and 23 weeks is increasing, and the attitudes of obstetricians and neonatologists are changing, leading to more active intervention and intensive care from the moment of birth in this gestational age range.[16] Hence the 24 week gestational age limit for abortion is based on data that was current in 1990, but it is now very out-of-date.

There are several factors which need to be taken into account when the survival of extremely premature infants is considered. First, it is well known that there is considerable inaccuracy in the determination of gestational age in clinical practice. It is generally accepted that errors of 1-2 weeks in gestational age are not uncommon. Hence the baby who is thought to be 22 weeks gestation may in fact be 24 weeks, and the baby who is thought to be 23 weeks may in fact be 25 weeks. This degree of inaccuracy is unavoidable, but it needs to be taken into account when changes in abortion legislation are being considered.

Second, there is clear evidence that the ethical attitudes of obstetric and neonatal staff make a significant difference to the chances of survival at the limits of viability. Some clinicians have a non-interventionist attitude when a mother goes into premature labour around the limits of viability. They may choose not to monitor the fetal heart rate during labour and may refuse to perform a caesarean section even if the fetus appears to be close to death. After delivery, they may withhold resuscitation unless the fetus is born in good condition. On the other hand, some clinicians will take an interventionist or active approach to the management of premature labour in order to maximise the chances of survival of the baby. It is not surprising that differences in the attitudes of clinicians will result in differences in survival statistics from different hospitals. A study from Sweden compared the outcome from two different regions of the country, in which neonatal staff were known to have different ethical attitudes to the care of extremely premature infants. The survival statistics in the interventionist hospitals were significantly improved compared with survival in the non-interventionist hospitals.[17]

Third, the division of survivors into 'healthy' and 'disabled' is overly simplistic. Several detailed and long-term follow-up studies of babies born at the limits of viability have been undertaken. These show that very approximately 40% of survivors do not have an identifiable disability, although on average they have lower cognitive scores compared with children born at term. Approximately 60% of survivors have some degree of disability.[18,19] However the term 'disability' when used medically applies to a very wide range of conditions. On the one hand it may refer to a child who has stiffness and spasticity in one limb but is otherwise completely healthy. On the other hand it may be used of a child with severe physical and learning difficulties who is completely dependent on others for all their care needs. Very approximately, 10-15% of survivors at the limits of viability are classified as severely disabled and dependent on others for all or most of their care needs.

It is also important to recognise that, although some survivors at the limits of viability do have significant disabilities, when they are asked to rate their own quality of life, studies have shown that they tend to rate it highly, and similar to those with no disabilities. For example one study investigated self-reported health status and health-related quality of life (HRQL) in a group of 140 adults born extremely premature compared with adults born at term.[20] Although health status was significantly worse in the adults who had been born premature, there was no significant difference in HRQL, and this finding remained when adults with neurological or learning difficulties were studied separately. It is clear that there is no simple correlation between the presence of a physical disability and a low self-assessment for quality of life. It must not be assumed that survival with disability equates inevitably with a low quality of life.

4. FETAL SENTIENCE AND THE CAPACITY TO FEEL PAIN

The concepts of fetal sentience and fetal pain are beset with philosophical and conceptual difficulties. It is not possible to have any certainty about the subjective experience of the human fetus, just as it is not possible to know what is the subjective experience of an animal who appears to be in pain. Yet, on the basis of the animal's behaviour, and the similarity of the mammalian central nervous system to ours, it has been generally assumed that, in the case of mammals, the experience of pain is real and intensely negative. This is the basis of animal welfare legislation in which, arguably, the UK leads the world. If an animal shows behaviour which appears to indicate the awareness of pain, then it is agreed that we should give the animal 'the benefit of the doubt', and take steps to ensure the eradication or mitigation of any possible painful sensations.

The question of fetal pain and our social and legal responses to it can never be resolved by scientific evidence alone. Our responses depend upon prior philosophical and social commitments to humane attitudes in the treatment of vulnerable sentient beings. It seems strange that in terms of legislation we appear to be more concerned about the protection of animals from pain than we are about human beings at an early stage of development.

In clinical practice, pain relief is given not when there is absolute scientific certainty that pain is present, but on the possibility that pain may be present. Therefore if pain is possible in the human fetus, it is logical that we should offer the fetus 'the benefit of the doubt' and provide pain relief.

Until the 1970s it was standard medical teaching that newborn babies could not experience pain, despite all the behavioural evidence to the contrary. Attention to pain relief in babies at the time was minimal, and surgical procedures were sometimes carried out with no pain relief.[21] Now there is abundant evidence about the reality of pain awareness and sensation in newborn babies down to the limits of viability at 22 and 23 weeks gestation. There is also clear evidence that painful stimuli can cause permanent changes in the developing nervous system.[22] It is now standard medical practice to assume that newborn babies born at all stages of gestation may experience severe pain, and hence attention to pain control is a major aspect of modern neonatal medicine and nursing.

A modern understanding of fetal development emphasises that the human fetus is not just a passive occupant of the womb. Instead the fetus is seen as a highly dynamic and interactive being that is in constant interaction with its environment. The fetus interacts with its intrauterine environment using the senses of hearing, vision, touch and taste, as well as physical orientation in space (proprioception).[23,24,25] This contrasts with the statement in a 2010 document, *Fetal Awareness*, produced by the RCOG, that "the fetus never experiences a state of true wakefulness in utero and is kept, by the presence of its chemical environment, in a continuous sleep-like unconsciousness or sedation".[26] On the basis of the available evidence this seems highly misleading and scientifically inaccurate.

The majority view of neuroscientists is that a functioning cerebral cortex is necessary before there can be any conscious awareness, including consciousness of pain. Since it is known that sensory pathways from the body and deeper parts of the brain are first connected to the cerebral cortex at approximately 23 or 24 weeks gestation, many scientists have therefore concluded that conscious awareness of pain is not possible before this point in fetal development.[27]

However, there are several strands of evidence that cast serious doubt on this conclusion:

First, as mentioned above on page 38, an active biological stress response to damaging stimuli, such as insertion of a needle, can be observed from 16 weeks onwards and a rise in stress hormones can be detected from 18 weeks onwards.[6] The presence of a biological or biochemical stress response does not *prove* that there is conscious awareness of pain but it is consistent with awareness of pain.

Second, there is growing evidence that structures in the deep brain regions called the thalamus and brainstem can be associated with conscious awareness of pain.[28,29] Hence it is possible that these structures enable awareness of pain in the developing fetus at an earlier gestational age before cortical connections are established.

Third, as mentioned previously, there is a population of brain cells which are called subplate neurons which establish a rich network of connections beneath the developing cerebral cortex.[30] This occurs from about 17 weeks of gestation, considerably earlier than 23-24 weeks when the first connections with the cerebral cortex are established. The precise function of the subplate neurons is not known but it is possible that they may lead to awareness of pain before the normal cortical connections are first established.

Fourth, extremely premature babies born at 22 and 23 weeks gestation appear to show conscious awareness and they may respond to painful stimulation, such as a heel-prick, with behavioural responses such as screwing up the face and breath-holding. The natural conclusion of these observations is that these extremely premature babies are capable of conscious awareness of pain, despite lack of functioning connections between the body and the cerebral cortex.

Fifth, in studies of premature babies it is known that there is often an increased and more prolonged response to painful stimuli in extremely preterm infants compared with more mature infants.[31]

Finally, newborn children who are born without a functioning cortex (rare congenital conditions known as anencephaly and hydranencephaly) may show evidence of pain awareness by screwing up their faces and crying in response to painful stimuli.[29] This again casts doubt on the majority view of neuroscientists that a functioning cerebral cortex is necessary before there can be any conscious awareness.

In summary, there are multiple lines of evidence which all point to the possibility of conscious awareness of pain in the fetus from 18 weeks of gestation or earlier. As discussed earlier, in clinical practice pain relief is given not when there is absolute scientific certainty that pain is present, but when there is a possibility that pain might be present. Since it is certainly possible that pain may be experienced in the human fetus, from 18 weeks of gestation or earlier, it is logical that we should offer the fetus 'the benefit of the doubt' and provide pain relief from 18 weeks if not earlier.

Conclusion

The current UK abortion limit of 24 weeks gestation is incompatible with continuing improvements in the survival of very premature babies at 22 and 23 weeks. There are strong reasons to reduce the time limit to avoid the abortion of infants who are capable of independent survival.

Endnotes

[1] It has become generally accepted that the correct English spelling for this word is fetus, since this is etymologically accurate – it most accurately represents the Greek word. The spelling 'foetus' is still commonly used but the diphthong oe is technically inaccurate. Oxford English Dictionary, Third Edition 2013.

[2] https://www.bpas.org/abortion-care/abortion-treatments/the-abortion-pill/abortion-pill-from-10-weeks-to-24-weeks/

[3] Abortion Statistics: England and Wales, 2018. Department of Health and Social Care

[4] *Termination of pregnancy for fetal abnormality in England, Wales and Scotland* Royal College of Obstetricians and Gynaecologists, Jan 1996.

[5] https://www.bpas.org/abortion-care/abortion-treatments/the-abortion-pill/feticide/

[6] Gitau R, Fisk NM, Glover V. Human fetal and maternal corticotrophin releasing hormone responses to acute stress. *Arch Dis Child Fetal Neonatal Ed* 2004;89:F29–32.

[7] Gibbins S, et al. Pain behaviours in Extremely Low Gestational Age infants. *Early Hum Dev.* 2008, 84:451-8.

[8] Holsti L, Grunau RE, Shany E. Assessing pain in preterm infants in the neonatal intensive care unit: moving to a 'brain-oriented' approach. *Pain Management.* 2011; 1: 171–179.

[9] Stewart AL, Reynolds EO, Lipscomb AP. Outcome for infants of very low birthweight: survey of world literature. *Lancet* 1981 May 9; 1(8228): 1038-40.

[10] European Community collaborative study of outcome of pregnancy between 22 and 28 weeks' gestation. Working Group on the Very Low Birthweight Infant. *Lancet.* 1990 Sep 29; 336(8718): 782-4.

[11] Riley K, Roth S, Sellwood M, Wyatt JS. Survival and neurodevelopmental morbidity at 1 year of age following extremely preterm delivery over a 20-year period: a single centre cohort study. *Acta Paediatrica.* 2008; 97: 159-65.

[12] Moore T et al. Neurological and developmental outcome in extremely preterm children born in England in 1995 and 2006: the EPICure studies. *BMJ* 2012; 345: e7961.

[13] Santhakumaran S et al. Survival of very preterm infants admitted to neonatal care in England 2008–2014: time trends and regional variation. *Arch Dis Child Fetal Neonatal Ed* 2018;103:F208–F215.

[14] Ibid.

[15] Norman M et al. Association Between Year of Birth and 1-Year Survival Among Extremely Preterm Infants in Sweden During 2004-2007 and 2014-2016.

[16] Framework for Practice on the Perinatal Management of Extreme Preterm Birth Before 27 Weeks of Gestation. British Association of Perinatal Medicine, October 2019.

[17] Håkansson S et al. Proactive Management Promotes Outcome in Extremely Preterm Infants: A Population-Based Comparison of Two Perinatal Management Strategies. *Pediatrics* 2004; 114: 58-64.

[18] Adams-Chapman I et al. Neurodevelopmental Impairment Among Extremely Preterm Infants in the Neonatal Research Network. *Pediatrics.* 2018; 141(5):e20173091.

[19] Serenius F et al, Neurodevelopmental Outcomes Among Extremely Preterm Infants 6.5 Years After Active Perinatal Care in Sweden. *JAMA Pediatr.* 2016; 170(10): 954-963.

[20] Saigal S et al. Self-perceived health-related quality of life of former extremely low birth weight infants at young adulthood. *Pediatrics.* 2006; 118(3): 1140-8.

[21] Hall RW, Anand KJ. Pain management in newborns. *Clin Perinatol.* 2014; 41(4): 895-924.

[22] Schwaller F1, Fitzgerald M. The consequences of pain in early life: injury-induced plasticity in developing pain pathways. *Eur J Neurosci.* 2014; 39(3): 344-52.

[23] Hepper PG. Fetal behaviour: why so sceptical? *Ultrasound Obstet Gynecol.* 1996; 8: 145-148.

[24] Lecanuet JP, Schaal B. Fetal sensory competencies. *Eur J Obstet Gynecol Reprod Biol.* 1996; 68(1-2): 1-23.

[25] Fagard J et al. Fetal Origin of Sensorimotor Behavior. *Frontiers Neurorobotics.* 2018; 12: 23.

[26] Royal College of Obstetricians and Gynaecologists. *Fetal Awareness: review of research and recommendations for practice.* March 2010.

[27] Ibid.

[28] Lowery CL et al. Neurodevelopmental changes of fetal pain. *Semin Perinatol.* 2007; 31(5): 275-82.

[29] Sekulic S et al. Appearance of fetal pain could be associated with maturation of the mesodiencephalic structures. *J Pain Res.* 2016; 9: 1031–1038.

[30] Ibid.

[31] Vinall J, Grunau RE. Impact of repeated procedural pain-related stress in infants born very preterm. *Pediatr Res.* 2014; 75: 584-7.

Riddhi's Story

I was in the UK on a student visa and I had a boyfriend. Neither of us was working.

When we found out I was pregnant, we knew we could not afford to bring a child into the world, so we decided that I would have an abortion.

When I went for my appointment at the abortion centre, as I entered the building, I was offered a leaflet. I took it and walked in the building and sat in the waiting area. At this time, I was feeling tired and didn't feel like reading. I also didn't feel well because I didn't want to abort the baby. My body was there, but my spirit was somewhere else, because I really didn't want to go through an abortion. Anyway, I began reading this leaflet. It mentioned that help could be given to women like me. I was feeling so sad because I didn't want to abort my baby.

My heart told me to leave the building and talk to the woman who had given me the leaflet. Her name was Janet. I wanted to save this child, because my heart was telling me that going through an abortion was wrong. Janet explained to me how help could be given. I would be helped with accommodation, if I needed it. As she told me about the help that was on offer, I cried. Janet told me not to worry and that everything could be taken care of. She invited me to chat over a coffee.

She then took me to the LIFE charity office in Hounslow. I told the lady there that I am living with my boyfriend and I am dependent on my dad. I also said my heart doesn't allow me to have an abortion, but I don't have a choice. It makes me sad that I couldn't afford to bring a child into the world. She told me the charity couldn't provide me with accommodation or money but could give food and nappies. As I needed somewhere to live, she recommended the Good Counsel Network (GCN), which was able to provide accommodation.

I saw Clare the next day at the GCN. When we met, she hugged me. She listened to me. I told her I was a student and didn't want to leave the course. Clare told me not to worry. I could be supported in my fees. My accommodation would also be paid for, along with food. In fact, they paid for my accommodation for over two years. This happened until we were able to find alternative living arrangements.

My right to stay in this country was based on holding a student visa. But the college I was registered at became unlisted. Clare helped me find another college, so that I could continue studying, and so that my student visa would not be at risk.

My son, David, is now five years old and is in his first year of primary school. Even now, the GCN are still giving me food vouchers to help us bring up our son. They are also helping us with clothes and books for the children. Since David's birth, I have given birth to a daughter, who is now three years old.

I am really grateful to God that I met Janet who offered me the leaflet. We are happy as a family.

Chapter Three

ABORTION AND QUESTIONS OF DISABILITY

Robert S. Harris

Introduction

The subject of abortion, and more specifically, its relationship to disability, cannot be considered on its own, separate from the complex web of law, ethics, culture and medical science that makes this a highly charged topic. Inevitably, the outcomes of what the law permits leave uncomfortable questions as to which kinds of human being qualify for entrance into the world. The word 'eugenics' carries associations with the Nazi vision of a master-race of 'perfect beings', achieved by eliminating those who were physically or mentally unfit, and so deemed unworthy to live. Today, though we do not live under the Nazi system, where State policy determines which humans are deemed 'unfit' to exist, we do use a rationale resting on another distinct ideology, not so very dissimilar from the notion of the perfect race.

The notion of creating a 'perfect race' is unsettling, but the intention behind it, and its possible outcome must be faced squarely. Debates about how current and future medical progress opens the door to 'designer babies' indicate another version of this attempt to achieve 'quality control' over which people are born. However we package these ideas, using socially 'respectable' terms, such as medical termination, a woman's 'right to choose', or reproductive rights, both the intention and the outcome remain the same: to exert premeditated control, so that 'imperfect' people are excluded from the human population. Lord Shinkwin, a disabled peer, has described abortion law as 'a licence to kill for the crime of being disabled'.[1]

During the passage of abortion legislation in 1966, Leo Abse, one of the leading liberal reformers of the Sixties, expressed deep concerns about the proposals when he said that no Member of Parliament:

> who acknowledges that life is our most precious gift can possibly view with enthusiasm a Bill whose declared object is to thwart the life of the unborn babe.[2]

Abse urged his fellow Parliamentarians to:

> believe that, ideally, a society should be such that every child, whether born fatherless, whether born handicapped, whether born in a palace or in a manger, should be received with warmth and be endowed with care. This is our starting point. Let no one suppose that a Bill of this kind can be a triumph for the community. There are societies which are impatient of doctrines which place the same ultimate worth on each personality. These societies are ready to rid themselves of all the weak, whom they regard as encumbrances. The Nazi society, the great life deniers, killed off the aged and the mentally backward...[3]

Our law allows disabled babies to be aborted. Unlike Nazi initiatives to kill off the disabled, nowadays it is women, in theory, who make their own choices about abortion.[4] According to evidence heard by a Parliamentary Inquiry into Abortion on the Grounds of Disability, duress from medical professionals to choose abortion, where a foetal disability is diagnosed, is apparently not uncommon.[5] The Inquiry found that in a 'considerable' number of cases, after parents were notified of this diagnosis, the presumption in the medical profession was that parents would choose abortion.[6] This violates principles promoted by the World Health Organisation (WHO), which declares that women hold the 'legal reproductive right to decide freely and responsibly without coercion' the number, spacing and timing of their children, including the 'information and means to do so.'[7] If such information is to be balanced and impartial, it must include everything connected to the diagnosis of disability, including the availability of support for parents who choose to raise a disabled child. Yet such points are absent from these WHO principles.

However we dress-up the practice, in order to alleviate our consciences, abortion performed on grounds of disability is often done because a disabled child fails parental expectations of the perfect baby. As in eugenics, the outcome is the same: to prevent people deemed as 'unfit' from taking their place in the human race. We may use what we think is a morally sound argument: 'the person will not have a reasonable quality of life, so why bring them into the world?' We also claim to be a non-judgmental society, accepting everyone, but this claim is not borne out by the facts. Granted, some abortions are done because the parents believe they will be unable to handle the emotional pressures of raising a disabled child. But the option of adoption surely avoids that.

Before we continue, let us consider the language used by abortion advocates. In public debates about abortion, perhaps one of the greatest obstacles to be observed is radical ideology. Radical ideology has no interest in facts, science, argument or evidence, though it will often disingenuously claim to respect all these things.

Its primary script is to repeat, in varying ways, its mantra about a woman's right to choose; its corrosive thinking is completely me-centred. This ideology has attempted to create a veneer of respectability by manipulating language, so that what is abhorrent is rebranded into something benign. Killing an unborn baby becomes 'a medical termination', or 'a woman's right to choose', or 'women's empowerment', or 'reproductive rights'.

The right of the baby to be born counts for nothing where dogma is king. In fact, dogma, when totally separated from the evidence, reason and argument, is very dangerous. Totalitarian regimes are replete with examples where State-established dogma justifies all kinds of unconscionable means, to ensure that certain ideological ends are realised. Totalitarian ideologues hate all moral or factual challenges that will upset, frustrate or oppose their perceived utopia. Killing innocent human life is wrong, they claim, but, in the case of abortion, there is no human person yet in being, so that makes abortion morally justified.

There is a well-known moral and legal anomaly at the heart of the medical culture of abortions. In one ward of a hospital, doctors work tirelessly to save a baby born prematurely, for example at 22 or 23 weeks, using state-of-the-art medical care to enhance the prospects of the child's survival and future health. In another ward, meanwhile, a baby of the same or similar age is intentionally killed, its mortal remains then being incinerated together with the hospital's daily output of medical waste. The essential difference in these cases is the arbitrary question of whether a woman's feelings are for or against her child being born. In effect, whether legal protections for the child come into play or not, depends upon the apparent randomness and haphazardness of what a woman chooses.

Human Rights: Whose Human Rights?

Abortion advocates love appealing to 'human rights' in their attempt to justify abortion, the so-called right of a woman to choose, to choose to destroy an innocent baby. Ideologues are so unhealthily preoccupied with this 'right to choose' that they remain silent about the competing right to life of the child.

In the 1959 Preamble of the UN Declaration on the Rights of the Child, it states:

> Whereas the child, by reason of his physical and mental immaturity, needs special safeguards and care, including appropriate legal protection, before as well as after birth.

This statement about the child before and after birth was repeated in the Preamble of the 1989 UN Convention on the Rights of the Child. Most human rights are conditional, meaning that they must be balanced against the demands of the competing rights and freedoms of others. This principle, sitting at the centre of human rights jurisprudence, is ignored in abortion ideology. This ideology's unjust, one-sided demand is that the desire of the woman for an abortion should trump the unborn child's right to life. It is only concerned about one party.

According to evidence presented to the Parliamentary Inquiry into Abortion on the Grounds of Disability,[8] international law is understood to protect the unborn child with disability in the Rome Statute of the International Criminal Court. In Article 6, acts of 'genocide' includes, among other things: 'Imposing measures intended to prevent births within the group.'[9] Along with Article 7, it makes clear that the acts in question must be committed with intent to destroy, at the very least, a part of a national, civilian population. This is all that is needed. Abortion advocates, in denying this application of Article 7, may argue that the relevant context is war and genocide. But aren't the disabled a target of annihilation, systematically overseen by the NHS in the name of so-called rights?

In actuality, we are erasing a section of our population, who are judged, if the blunt truth be stated, as not being worthy and qualified to be born. All this in a society where, oddly enough, many pro-abortion, feminist voices find the idea of aborting a foetus on grounds of gender, abhorrent. This oddity in reasoning rests on the incoherent belief that gender-based abortion (where a female foetus is aborted) is an act of violence or an attack on women, and/or is offensive to women's dignity. Yet the advocates holding passionately to this view likewise claim there is no human person in the womb, the basis upon which they justify a woman's 'right to choose' more generally. This logically indefensible position renders an abortion for reasons of unwanted gender, abhorrent, but fails to take the same moral position for abortion on grounds of abnormality. If terminating a foetus for reasons of unwanted gender is an attack on women, why is termination of a disabled foetus not an attack on disabled people? This incongruous, disjointed thinking is embedded into the law. Abortion, if done for reasons of gender (also known as 'sex selection'), remains illegal, unless based on a sex-linked inherited medical condition.[10] In this case, where the condition renders the child liable to becoming disabled, this is one of several conditions that makes abortion based on gender lawful.[11]

The main body of law in this country is the 1967 Abortion Act. It is worth noting, firstly, that the Act did not decriminalise abortion.[12] Abortion remains a criminal offence, but as long as the parties comply with the statutory conditions, then they are not subject to criminal prosecution. But that is not the extent of the issue. The law is worded in such a manner that evidently allows loopholes, so that it can be used and abused in ways never, apparently, intended by David Steel and his co-sponsors of abortion reform.

Subject to the law's stipulations, women are able to abort their unwanted pregnancies with minimal obstacles but the child's inherent right to life is blatantly excluded from abortion legislation. Though it may be popularly assumed that a woman has a 'human right' to have an abortion,[13] Human Rights charters, such as the Universal Declaration of Human Rights (1948) and the European Convention on Human Rights (1950) do not in fact contain any such right.[14]

Pre-1967 Historical Highlights

A key factor in the development of abortion law was the creation of the Abortion Law Reform Association (ALRA) as long ago as 1936. According to the Institute of Contemporary British History, this group was made up of "socialist-feminists" and was 'never a mass or even particularly large organisation, but the cause of legal abortion until 1967 owes everything to this small band of activists.'[15] Madeleine Simms, who worked as an activist with the ALRA, was asked by a disabled activist whether disabled people were ever consulted during their lobbying and campaigning work of the 1960s. She asked:

> I am all for a woman's right to choose to have an abortion or not to have an abortion, and I want to ask you, in the 1960s, did any of you consult with disabled people whether they wanted not to exist simply on the grounds of being disabled and what consultation has been done with disabled people on whether they should have the right to exist? Again, I will say, the 1967 Abortion Act was progressive in a woman's right to have a termination but I think there needs to be a distinction between is it a woman's right to pick and choose the type of baby she gives birth to as well?[16]

Madeleine Simms responded:

> I think the answer to that is we didn't consult anybody and if you believe in a woman's right to choose, then this must be one of the aspects that it is the woman's right to choose about.[17]

The disabled activist then went on to ask one of the big elephant-in-the-room questions. Should a woman be permitted to abort on grounds of gender and ethnicity? We have to acknowledge the honesty of the former ALRA activist when she expressed her belief that even gender and ethnicity should not be bars to a termination.

The idea of abortion on grounds of ethnicity[18] rightly shocks right-minded people, but abortion advocates argue that it is permissible to abort an unborn child who is disabled (or is at risk of becoming so) because we're not, they insist, talking about an actual person. Why therefore, following these morally and logically flawed steps of reasoning, is it wrong and abhorrent to abort on grounds of ethnicity – or even gender?

This leaves unresolved moral, and indeed, legal questions. At the heart of this pro-choice ideology, there are these gaping problems that have no credible intellectual defence; they are defended by an appeal to dogma and ideology.

Logically, the argument that a woman has the right to choose, coupled with the belief that there is no human being in existence in the womb, leads to the conclusion that it is not morally objectionable to abort on grounds of disability.

But when the foetus is of a gender or ethnicity not wanted by the mother – what then? Pro-choice activists frequently deny that a woman's right to choose extends to gender- or ethnicity-based abortions, because that is rightly deemed offensive to women generally and to different ethnic groups. But the same tolerance of difference and inclusivity does not, seemingly, extend to those suffering from disability. Why the anomaly?

Disability and Abortion: Legal Background

During the Second Reading of the Medical Termination Bill (as it was then called), David Steel told Parliament:

The difficulty in drafting a Bill of this kind is to decide how and where to draw the line. We want to stamp out the back-street abortions, but it is not the intention of the Promoters of the Bill to leave a wide open door for abortion on request.[19]

Eventually, lines were indeed drawn, between on the one hand allowing a child to be born, and on the other deciding those pregnancies that could be lawfully terminated. Abortion activists have long argued that the requirement for compliance with the conditions as laid down in law provides safeguards against misapplication or abuse. But in truth, as we will see, certain lines that were drawn in the legislation have been trampled on, making a mockery of the rule of law.

David Steel went on to say that:

We have to avoid in the Bill wording which is so restrictive as not to have the effect which we are seeking—namely, the ending of the back-street abortions.[20]

Steel was warning those with reservations about the Bill not to narrow the legal scope of abortion because this would undermine the intended goal.

The law in the UK[21] accords no human rights to the unborn child at any stage of gestation. However, the unborn child is not without some, albeit very limited protections. For example, the law presumes that from twenty-four weeks, the foetus or unborn child has acquired viability and therefore can only be aborted in stricter, more limited circumstances. Viability means that if the child were born, it could survive, independent of its mother, with the necessary medical support. Only when the child is physically separated from the mother, by having the umbilical cord cut, is he or she treated as a legal person, eligible for human rights and equality protections.

Disability is one of the nine protected characteristics in the Equality Act 2010, alongside gender, sexual orientation, marital status, religion and so forth. But a child only gets protected by the law when outside the womb. When inside, at any point in the nine-month period, for reasons of disability, the child can be destroyed.

The law governing the area of disability and the unborn child is found in the Abortion Act 1967, section 1 (1) (d), sometimes referred to as either the 'foetal disability clause' or the 'foetal abnormality clause'. There is no time limit for an abortion when:

> there is a substantial risk that if the child were born it would suffer from such physical or mental abnormalities as to be seriously handicapped.

It is a matter of broad opinion and tense debate as to what counts as a 'substantial risk', 'physical or mental abnormalities' and 'seriously handicapped'. When Parliament debated these terms in 1966 and 1967, there was great uncertainty as to their meaning, and the many doubts that were cast then have never been resolved. It remains a matter of great controversy whether the law should permit abortion on the basis of the child being physically or mentally abnormal or disabled, or, in the language of the Abortion Act, 'handicapped'.[22]

Controversially, unborn children found to have developed a cleft palate or cleft lip have been aborted, despite this abnormality being capable of post-natal surgical correction.[23]

Statutory Law

Until the Abortion Act 1967, the Infant Life (Preservation) Act 1929 provided that:

> any person who, *with intent to destroy the life of a child capable of being born alive*, by any wilful act *causes a child to die before it has an existence independent of its mother*, shall be guilty of felony, to wit, of child destruction, and shall be liable on conviction thereof on indictment to penal servitude for life.[24] (emphasis added)

The 1929 Act was designed to 'amend the law with regard to the destruction of children at or before birth'.[25] It recognised that a child was viable from twenty-eight weeks, that is, the 'child [was considered] capable of being born alive.'[26]

It is important to note that in 1990, new legislation made two big changes in abortion law: it reduced the upper limit of viability to twenty-four weeks, and permitted terminations in cases of disability, without any time limit. Thus, the 1967 Act was amended.

One doctor, when offering testimony to the Parliamentary Inquiry into Abortion on the Grounds of Disability, said:

> Section 1(1)(d) can be seen as an anomaly in the broader context of legislative measures to prevent abortions, as it affords fetuses with a potential disability a different, lower level of protection than they would otherwise have but for their 'diagnosis'.[27]

Another doctor who gave evidence to this Inquiry gave a striking insight into how people generally consider the ultrasound image, and what this perspective tells us about how disabled people are adversely judged. She said:

> it is common now that ultrasound images are included in baby albums. At a certain stage of development, the person born without disabilities will be looking back at an image of what many people would clearly think of as 'themselves at an earlier stage', and after 24 weeks' gestation, this will be a stage where they were legally protected. The person born with disabilities will be looking back at 'themselves at an earlier stage', but at no point of gestation was their life protected by the law concerning termination of pregnancy.[28]

These points raise serious moral and legal questions. If the unborn child shows signs of a disability, that life is not given the same protection, potentially, as that enjoyed by unborn children without disabilities. This exposes a serious conflict within a society that makes so much of protecting disadvantaged or vulnerable groups in the name of equality. In modern society we subscribe to the idea that, as human beings, we are all equal, each of us part of the diversity that makes up the world, regardless of ability or capacity. How does the law in the area of abortion reflect this principle? Plainly, it does not.

Is the law outdated and in need of reform?

Since 1990, medical advances have led to further improvements in the post-natal care of prematurely born children. Figures for surviving preterm babies provide a compelling case for reducing the legal time limit to below 24 weeks (the time limit for most abortions). Also, it is a common error to assume that all or most pre-term babies are or will become disabled.

According to its *Framework for Practice*,[29] the British Association of Perinatal Medicine (BAPM) notes that at "all gestational ages, survival rates show ongoing improvement".[30] It adds that international data shows a trend towards babies surviving at 22 weeks, where rates of survival are at approximately one-third, when active treatment is provided. While babies born prematurely do not automatically develop disabilities, the guidance states:

> Assessment of the risk of severely disabling conditions among survivors is fraught with difficulty, not least differences in individual views about *acceptable levels of disability*. What for one individual or family may be an acceptable outcome may not be acceptable for another. For decisions about provision of potentially life-sustaining treatment, the ethically relevant consideration is the risk of disabilities that could affect *whether it is in the baby's best interests to survive* and thus risk assessment should focus on the most severe disabilities.[31] [emphasis added]

When the BAPM speaks of 'acceptable levels of disability' and 'whether it is in the baby's best interests to survive', it becomes a self-appointed god, with the power to make life or death decisions.

Approximately one in seven children, born at 24 weeks gestation, are at risk of severe impairment.[32] This means that six out of every seven children born at 24 weeks do not develop severe impairment.

At 23 weeks gestation, survival rates diminish to 25%.[33] This translates as twenty-five people in every hundred living in the world born at 23 weeks gestation, who might otherwise have been killed by abortion because the mother was not willing to take the risk of having a severely impaired child.

'Risk' of abnormality: how is the law interpreted and applied?

With the wide range of diverse and conflicting opinions that were aired in Parliament about the meaning of the words in section 1 (1) (d) – the 'foetal disability clause' in the 1967 Abortion Act – unresolved and pertinent questions remain as to the legal meaning of: 'substantial risk', 'physical or mental abnormalities' and 'seriously handicapped'. It should be noted that the potential breadth and vagueness of these phrases allow the law to be applied liberally, even abusively. Therefore, a decision to abort can be weighed in favour of a woman seeking a termination on questionable legal grounds, or for reasons that are morally dubious or shallow. This means that an abortion could be done on a ground that was not intended (at least not blatantly) by David Steel and his promoters in Parliament. The criminal law in the field of abortion is thus relegated, potentially, to an exercise in ticking the 'right box', while defying the underlying spirit of the law, and the purpose for which it was originally intended and drafted.

During the Parliamentary debates of Steel's Abortion Bill, Sir John Hobson, a former Attorney General who was not an outright opponent of the Bill, had this to say about the possibility of risk that a child may be born with a physical or mental abnormality, and who may also be seriously handicapped:

> This raises a very different combination of conceptions. First, there is the question of the seriousness of the risk, and, secondly, there is the risk of serious deformity. These are two quite different subjects.[34]

Another MP, Kevin McNamara, said:

> The phrases which are used 'substantial risk', 'seriously handicapped' — are difficult to interpret and are incapable of precise definition. What exactly does 'substantial risk' mean?[35]

He went on to say:

> It is almost impossible to give a definition. How are we to measure this? Where do we draw the line?[36]

In his speech, McNamara referred to Lord Brain's commentary published in the British Medical Journal. This was a detailed response to a Bill sponsored by Lord Silkin[37] (a predecessor of Steel's Bill).

This earlier Bill contained a clause largely similar in wording to the current law but including also the idea of 'any prospect of reasonable enjoyment of life.' Under the Silkin Bill, abortion on grounds of disability would have been lawful when:

> there is a substantial risk that if the child were born it would
> suffer from such physical or mental abnormalities as to deprive
> it of any prospect of reasonable enjoyment of life.

Lord Brain, a leading medical authority of his day who became President of the Royal College of Physicians, asked: 'how great a degree of probability of abnormality is required to justify the termination of the pregnancy, and the further question, by whom this probability is to be estimated.'[38] He questioned the level of accuracy, when estimating the risk of abnormality, which he thought 'must vary greatly in different circumstances.'

Lord Brain anticipated the loophole that the current law provides: 'if the mother's mental health is seriously threatened by the fear that the unborn child may be abnormal, the pregnancy could [still] be terminated... without the need for a precise assessment of that risk.' This ground in Silkin's Bill provided that abortion could be lawful if:

> continuance of the pregnancy would involve serious risk to the life
> or grave injury to the health, whether physical or mental, of the
> pregnant woman, whether before, at, or after the birth of the child.[39]

Reflecting on the debate of Silkin's Bill, Lord Brain said he felt disappointment that: 'The most fundamental question of all was hardly discussed: how does one decide what physical or mental abnormalities deprive a child of any prospect of reasonable enjoyment of life?' The current law is silent on cases that 'deprive a child of any prospect of reasonable enjoyment of life'. But it is not difficult to interpret section 1 (1) (d), the foetal disability clause, to include the meaning of the child being deprived of 'any prospect of reasonable enjoyment of life'. By leaving the application of the foetal disability clause open to wide interpretation and the varying judgments of individual doctors, the current law fails to address this fundamental moral question.

During the progress of debates on Steel's Medical Termination Bill, some MPs attempted to offer reassurance. Their essential argument was that it would be for doctors alone to decide on risk in a given situation, and how to measure it. Yet others could foresee how this would create problems for doctors; surely it was for Parliament to make the law, and for doctors to be guided by it, they argued. But how could doctors be confidently guided by it, when what the law allows is open to such wide interpretation?

In fact, it was intentional to give doctors a wide discretion, as David Steel made clear. A range of legally and morally contentious scenarios exist, when the foetal disability clause can be invoked.

First, in the absence of a risk of 'serious' abnormality, abortion may still be permitted but authorised under a different clause. The risk of serious disability may be small or very remote, but no offence is committed if authorisation is made by two registered medical practitioners who believe in good faith that:

> continuance of the pregnancy would involve risk, greater than if the
> pregnancy were terminated, or injury to the physical or mental health
> of the pregnant woman or any existing children of her family.[40]

In these kinds of cases, a woman may be motivated to abort *because* of a disability that is not considered 'serious' by the doctor. Yet, the authorising doctors need only anticipate a (theoretical) risk of 'injury' to the woman's future mental health if she carries her child to term, for the abortion to be technically legal. In practice, only one doctor will meet the woman and gather the information, and once he or she approves, a second authorising doctor tends to sign-off this approval without having ever met the patient. This is a time-bound clause, where the abortion must be done within 24 weeks. As noted earlier, where a woman relies on the foetal disability clause alone, there is no time limit.

'The social clause' In what is sometimes called 'the social clause', there only needs to be a risk that, *if* the pregnancy is continued, then various adverse outcomes *may follow* in terms of the woman's mental or physical health, or for her existing children – but these outcomes could be quite hypothetical, and not actually reflecting the presenting facts. This is enough, however, to tick the box and be seen to be legally compliant, even though the real reason for termination may be that of not wanting a child with small imperfections.

With the risk of serious abnormality, is the abnormality merely possible, or is it probable or is it actual? These are some of the questions that were raised by concerned Parliamentarians during the passage of David Steel's Bill yet, confronted by difficult cases, we are none the wiser today as to the actual meaning and application of this part of the legislation.

Post-abortion risk to a woman's mental health In cases generally, where the social clause is applied, something that is not commonly brought to a woman's attention is the post-abortion risk to her mental health. There is a growing body of credible evidence showing that a woman may actually put her future mental health at risk, if she has an abortion.[41] While the global medical profession is yet to achieve a consensus, existing findings linking abortions to subsequent mental health problems should not be excluded from the information women are given. To intentionally keep women in the dark about possible health outcomes is to deny them a comprehensive knowledge of their range of options and risks.

Can risk of disability be quantified? There are cases when the ultrasound fails to show evidence of any disability but genetic tests indicate a potential risk of postnatal abnormality. This is a judgment call in which doctors will consider the statistical probability of a postnatal disability developing. Since the law fails to stipulate how to apply this knowledge of risk, doctors will follow their own understanding of what is treated as 'serious' or 'abnormal' and what constitutes a 'disability'.

In this case of aborting a disabled foetus, there is arguably a potential violation of the spirit of the law. Despite the intendedly wide latitude afforded by Steel and his sponsors, was it really the intention of Parliament for abortions to be done for reasons not permitted by the

Act? Clearly not. As noted above, Steel stated, "...it is not the intention of the Promoters of the Bill to leave a wide open door for abortion on request." He added, "We have to avoid in the Bill wording which is so restrictive as not to have the effect which we are seeking – namely, the ending of the back-street abortions."

In this area there are several serious problems, for which medically objective answers may be elusive. Legal answers, however, can be created or imagined because the law's provisions are wide enough in scope. This wide breadth means that up to the 24-week limit, there might as well, effectively, be no actual limit to a woman's demand for an abortion,[42] where the possibility of a mental health 'risk', however remote, is relied upon.

Ultimately, unless the risk is properly quantified, the law's broad latitude allows for wide-ranging interpretation and application.

A charter for eugenics A number of theories have been put forward as to why the law allows abortion for reasons of disability. Some people claim that it is not about disrespecting disabled people, but about whether a woman is psychologically ready for the challenges she will face as the mother of a disabled child. In any event, they remind us, the foetus is not yet a person. The effect (regardless of the motives for terminating disabled foetuses) seems to be: lawful abortions done under the foetal disability clause provide a charter for eugenics. The claim that there is equality of all people, especially those who are disadvantaged, vulnerable or marginalised, effectively becomes one of the modern myths of society.

Another of society's myths is that we don't judge others, a principle taking the form of two questions: Who are we to judge? Who are we to condemn? If we apply the 'do not judge' injunction to this debate about having an abortion on account of foetal disability, there is a clear moral conflict. If we are to avoid judging the value inherent in human life, disabled or able-bodied, it means we cannot cast aside disabled foetuses, as being effectively unfit for birth. Another common argument supporting the destruction of disabled children is that the child won't have a quality life. When interviewed by the writer some time ago, Baroness Warnock, moral philosopher and authority on bioethics, said that some children, if born, won't have a reasonable quality of life, implying that this gives total justification for abortion. But what qualifies any mere mortal to decide this question?

If we take it upon ourselves to make these moral judgements about quality of life, it opens the door to wider questions of whether infanticide may be permissible. If justification for abortion is premised on a woman's choice to do what she wants with her body, combined with the assumption that the foetus is not yet a human person, then is permitting infanticide any different? It has been argued that newborns, for example, lack personhood because they lack self-awareness, so killing them may be morally justified. But on this basis, such thinking would logically open the way for killing people in a permanent coma, since they too may be deemed incapable of self-awareness.

Ground E Abortions

Ground E abortions refers to the foetal disability clause. As noted above, the basis of this is section 1 (1) (d) of the 1967 Abortion Act, which gives permission for an abortion when there is a 'substantial risk that if the child were born it would suffer from such physical or mental abnormalities as to be seriously handicapped.'

In 2018, of the 3269 abortions performed under Ground E in England and Wales, the principal medical conditions were:

Chromosomal abnormalities: 33%

Congenital malformations of the nervous system: 21%

Other congenital malformations: 27%

Other conditions: 18%.[43]

The criteria used to classify these medical conditions is the International Classification of Diseases, produced by the World Health Organisation.[44]

In the same year, women aged 35 and above constituted the highest age group for Ground E abortions: 1272 from a total of 3269 (39%). In contrast, there were 69 Ground E abortions for women aged under 20 (0.3%).[45] There were 618 reported cases of Down's syndrome (19% of Ground E abortions), the most commonly reported chromosomal abnormality.[46]

Of 111 selective abortions performed in 2018, that is, when the number of foetuses is reduced, 86% of these terminations were under Ground E.[47] A selective abortion involves aborting one or more of the foetuses developing in the womb. The reasons include wanting to limit the number of children born to a family, or deeming the foetus undesirable because it carries possible or confirmed abnormal characteristics.

What is the position of the RCOG?

As to what constitutes a serious foetal abnormality, in the context of abortion, the Royal College of Obstetricians and Gynaecologists (RCOG) suggests, in a report from 2010, that when interpreting 'serious handicap', at a minimum, it "would require the child to have physical or mental disability which would cause significant suffering or long-term impairment of their ability to function in society."[48] But are there objective criteria for the doctor to discuss with the mother, on the basis of which a decision will be made, as to whether the pregnancy will be allowed to continue or not?

In the same report, it is stated:

> There is no legal definition of substantial risk. Whether a risk will be regarded as substantial may vary with the seriousness and consequences of the likely disability. Likewise, there is no legal definition of serious handicap. An assessment of the seriousness of a fetal abnormality should be considered on a case-by-case basis, taking into account all available clinical information.[49]

The RCOG report claims to be not prescriptive but explanatory, by providing information 'to assist doctors and other health professionals to support women and their families when a fetal abnormality is diagnosed and to help women to decide, within the constraints of the law, whether or not to have the pregnancy terminated.'[50] Evidence from the Parliamentary Inquiry, noted earlier, suggests this recommendation is followed inadequately, if at all.

Further investigations are necessary to establish the scale of this non-compliance. Only a Public Inquiry could muster the resources to inquire into nationwide practices.

Disabled Children: Informing and Supporting Parents

When parents are informed that their child *in utero* is showing signs, or is at risk, of developing a disability, who is in control of the decision to abort? What relevant information are parents given about all their options, enabling them to reach an informed choice about the pregnancy? (It should be noted that fathers have no legal rights in abortion decisions.) Are the relevant medical professionals trained in providing information about the range of options available to families who are given the diagnosis of a disability?

According to evidence given to the Parliamentary Inquiry into Abortion on the Grounds of Disability (also known as the Commission):

> Many respondents reported to the Commission about their experiences of facing the discovery of a fetal disability. There was a common message that most parents are steered towards abortion and feel that they do not receive adequate information about other options, including palliative care after birth and adoption, as well as the reality of living with a child with a disability. Evidence from witnesses highlighted the varying and inconsistent approaches towards informing, counselling and supporting parents in different clinical settings when fetal disability is discovered.[51]

The Commission's recommendations[52] include:

• The option of palliative care should be on offer to all parents who are considering their decisions after being informed about a foetal disability (funding palliative care for newborns should be increased);

• Parents should be encouraged and supported to consider adoption as a "positive option"; after their discovery of a foetal disability, it should be best practice for parents to receive practical and balanced information before they leave hospital (including the offer of information from disability groups, and, contact with families that include a child with a similar condition) so that they can make an informed decision;

• Best practice guidelines should be created, covering training and practice in the counselling of families who face a foetal disability diagnosis;

• Guidelines to be established that cover training for medical professionals on the "practical realities of the lives of children" living with conditions screened through ante-natal tests;

• It is "imperative" to improve adequate and long-term care and support in readiness for both the disabled and their carers.

More generally, the Commission also recommends a radical overhaul of the 1967 Act where disability is concerned. It proposes:

• A third medical practitioner to sign the abortion form (the law currently stipulates two), to authorize that the family has received correct information and support enabling them to make an informed decision, and to confirm that the abortion complies with the statutory criteria; in one submission to the Commission, it was further proposed that the third signatory should be "separate" from the two doctors;[53]

• For Parliament to review the question of allowing abortions on foetal disability grounds and, how the law applies to a foetus above 24 weeks, that is, the "age of viability". Parliament should consider either: equalising the time limit for abortion when based on grounds of foetal disability, making it 24 weeks as it is for non-disabled children, instead of up to birth, or, repealing section 1 (1) (d).[54]

A majority of the Commission's witnesses found the discrepancy between the two time limits, for disabled and able-bodied babies, to be discriminatory.

Lord Shinkwin tabled a written question for the Government, which included, amongst other points, asking if steps had been taken to ensure that issues highlighted by this Inquiry had been addressed:

> in particular the finding that many parents are steered towards abortion and feel that they do not receive adequate information about other options.[55]

On behalf of the Government, Lord Prior responded to this part of the question saying:

> Guidance from the Royal College of Obstetricians and Gynaecologists makes it clear that women and their partners should receive appropriate information and support from a properly trained multidisciplinary team, who must adopt a supportive and non-judgemental approach.

It is unsatisfactory for a health minister to cite established guidance uncritically, in the face of challenging evidence indicating that its compliance is insufficient and lacks impartiality.

It is also professionally and morally wrong when doctors place any kind of pressure on women to choose abortion, in circumstances where the unborn child is thought to be at risk of disability. That such outcomes are being reported indicates, in any event, that the system is in need of review. The original idea, debated in Parliament in the lead up to the 1967 Act, was that it was the woman who should make the decision about whether to proceed with her pregnancy or not. The law was set up so that, while it is the doctor who assesses the legal and medical aspects underpinning authorization, it is implicit that this happens at the woman's prior initiative requesting it.

A Public Inquiry? Were it to be established, a Public Inquiry would need to be tasked with at least three primary objectives. First, it should study the situations and scale of professional abuses where women are placed under pressure to abort, not just in situations of foetal disability but in other scenarios too (except where a pregnant woman is at risk of death or life-threatening injury). Second, it should propose forms of best practice, ensuring that women are fully counselled and informed of all their options, including palliative care and the possibility of offering their child, if unwanted, for adoption. Third, it should assess the weaknesses and shortcomings in the current welfare system, and propose radical solutions to support families faced with the financial and emotional pressures of bringing up a disabled child.

For this Inquiry to offer meaningful results, it must be premised on two principles: first, the inherent equality of all disabled people, and secondly their intrinsic worth. Anything short of these principles would inevitably send the message that the worth and dignity of human beings is founded on their level of utility and their capacity to perform and achieve. It is important to note that when able-bodied people become incapacitated through accident or illness, we, as a society, do not see them as less valuable and worthy of life, by comparison with those retaining full capacities. In the same way, disabled individuals about to make their entrance into the world are equally deserving of respect and protection.

Concluding Summary

When performed on the grounds of disability, abortion is often chosen because parental expectations of having a 'perfect' baby are not being fulfilled. The practice of denying the right to life of those individuals who, *in utero*, show signs of, or are at risk of, developing a disability, contradicts society's claim to be non-judgmental and accepting of all people. This is a form of eugenics, performed under the name of 'reproductive rights' or a 'woman's right to choose'.

While the law denies personhood to the child *in utero*, this is incongruent with the fact that hospital staff will do their utmost to save the life of a prematurely born baby of less than 24 weeks, while in the same hospital, a child of the same age can be legally aborted. This moral and legal incoherence reveals an arbitrary and random approach, with the result that some children are denied legal and equality protections; their fate is sealed.

Generally, abortion is not legally permitted in cases of unwanted sex, and never on grounds of ethnicity, yet disability, currently, does qualify as a condition. This legal and moral anomaly places a disabled child *in utero* in a unique risk category, depriving him or her of the protections (albeit limited by statutory conditions) otherwise afforded to non-disabled children. The foetal disability clause must therefore be reviewed. A Parliamentary Inquiry has called for this clause either to be repealed or to be aligned with the 24-week time limit for other abortions.

In the light of the evidence, it is an error to assume that all or most pre-term babies will become disabled. Since the law was last updated in 1990, medical advances have now brought about further improvements in the post-natal care of prematurely born children. An increase in survival rates provides a compelling case for reducing the legal time limit to below 24 weeks (the time limit for most abortions).

There is no medical consensus as to what constitutes a 'substantial risk that if the child were born it would suffer from such physical or mental abnormalities as to be seriously handicapped'. This lack of definition opens the law to abuse, thus violating the apparent intentions of Parliament.

Evidence indicates that there is a presumption in the medical profession that abortion will be chosen, following a diagnosis of foetal disability. In cases when women are placed under any degree of duress to abort, the scale of malpractice should be examined by a public inquiry, also to be tasked with proposing protocols of best practice for parental counselling, following the diagnosis of a foetal disability. Reports of women being pressured, or expected, to abort because of a diagnosis of foetal disability raise serious questions about whether, and how, professional recommendations are actually being followed. There is also evidence of parents not being properly informed, if at all, of all their options, and of women not being given the counselling that would fully empower them to make informed decisions. It is surely time that society should recognise the hypocrisy of its judgmental approach, condemning the disabled and disadvantaged to death, and act to defend those who cannot defend themselves.

Endnotes

---

[1] https://www.telegraph.co.uk/news/2017/03/10/tory-peer-lord-shinkwin-warns-britains-abortion-laws-licence/

[2] Medical Termination of Pregnancy Bill, HC Deb 22 July 1966 vol 732 col 1147.

[3] Ibid.

[4] Exceptions to this rule are when the pregnant woman is herself lacking mental capacity of the kind where a court decides an abortion or sterilisation is necessary.

See: https://www.telegraph.co.uk/news/health/news/7772172/Secret-Court-of-Protection-can-order-abortions-and-sterilisations-of-mentally-ill-patients.html.

For a recent successful court challenge against an abortion being done by court order, see: https://www.theguardian.com/world/2019/jun/24/catholic-church-hits-out-at-court-over-abortion-ruling

[5] *Parliamentary Inquiry into Abortion on the Grounds of Disability*, chaired by Fiona Bruce MP, July 2013, see pp. 24-25.

[6] Ibid.

[7] https://www.who.int/health-topics/abortion#tab=tab_1

[8] p. 11.

[9] https://www.icc-cpi.int/resourcelibrary/official-journal/rome-statute.aspx

[10] See letter from the Chief Medical Officer, Professor Dame Sally Davies, Department of Health, 23 February 2012.

[11] Ibid.

[12] Under the Offences Against the Person Act 1861 (ss 58 and 59) abortion remains a criminal offence.

[13] 'The Guardian view on abortion: protecting a human right', 12 May 2019. https://www.theguardian.com/commentisfree/2019/may/12/the-guardian-view-on-abortion-protecting-a-human-right

[14] While no globally ratified human rights charter contains a right to abortion *per se*, UN agencies do make claims about such a right. For example, the United Nations Population Fund 'calls for the realization of reproductive rights for all and supports access to a wide range of sexual and reproductive health services – including voluntary family planning, maternal health care and comprehensive sexuality education.' https://www.unfpa.org/about-us

Note that 'reproductive rights' or 'reproductive health' refers to, among other things, abortion.

The World Health Organisation also declares: 'The right to legal and safe abortion' is one of the 'fundamental reproductive rights'.

https://www.who.int/health-topics/abortion#tab=tab_1

[15] *The Abortion Act 1967*, ed. Michael D. Kandiah and Gillian Staerck, ICBH Witness Seminar Programme, Institute of Contemporary British History, 2002, p. 16.

[16] p. 58.

[17] Ibid.

[18] While the Abortion Act 1967 makes no mention of ethnicity, the stated conditions, providing for when an abortion is lawful, would impliedly prohibit an abortion done on grounds of ethnicity. In theory, an abortion done under the reason of risk to the woman's future mental health could apparently make it technically lawful, albeit an abuse of statutory provision. This has never been tested in a court and in any event, given the clear statutory conditions of what constitutes lawful abortions, any judge who rendered ethnicity as a lawful reason would be acting *ultra vires*.

[19] HC Deb 22 July 1966 vol 732 col 1075.

[20] Ibid.

[21] This covers England, Wales and Scotland. In October 2019, the Northern Ireland (Executive Formation etc) Act 2019 was passed. This Act decriminalized abortion in the province, setting in motion the most liberal abortion regime in the UK.

[22] Long since the abortion legislation passed in 1967, fashions have changed in language. 'Handicapped' as a term has been replaced by 'disabled'. The new usage appears to be based on the fact of derogatory connotations that became associated with 'handicapped'. It is worth noting that 'disabled' is also an imperfect term, suggesting, as it does, a person who lacks ability. Yet, many disabled people have much to offer across the wide spectrum of 'ability' and the term is therefore unhelpful in conveying the full and varying potential of all those individuals with disabilities.

[23] See: https://www.nhs.uk/conditions/Cleft-lip-and-palate/

[24] The reference to 'penal servitude for life' is interpreted as a reference to imprisonment for life or any shorter term; see the Criminal Justice Act 1948 (c. 58), s. 1(1).

[25] http://www.legislation.gov.uk/ukpga/Geo5/19-20/34/introduction

[26] Section 1 (2).

[27] *Parliamentary Inquiry into Abortion on the Grounds of Disability*, chaired by Fiona Bruce MP, July 2013, p. 9.

[28] Ibid.

[29] Perinatal Management of Extreme Preterm Birth before 27 weeks of gestation: A Framework for Practice, British Association of Perinatal Medicine, October 2019. https://www.bapm.org/resources/80-perinatal-management-of-extreme-preterm-birth-before-27-weeks-of-gestation-2019.

[30] Ibid., p. 7.

[31] Ibid.

[32] Ibid., p. 8.

[33] Ibid.

[34] HC Deb 22 July 1966 vol 732 col 1134.

[35] HC Deb 22 July 1966 vol 732 col 1127.

[36] Ibid

[37] 1965-66.

[38] *Medical Issues in Abortion Law Reform*, BMJ, 19 March 1966, 727-729.

[39] Abortion Bill, HL Deb 03 February 1966 vol 272 col 491.

[40] See section 1 (1) (a).

[41] See *Abortion and Women's Health* by Dr Gregg Pike, a medical researcher, published by SPUC, updated 2017. (https://www.spuc.org.uk › 750-abortion-and-womens-health-april-2017-pdf)
See also "Abortion and Mental Health: What do the Studies Say?" by Robert S. Harris, in *Relationships and Sex Education: The Way Forward,* a Report from the Lords and Commons Family and Child Protection Group, September 2018, published by Voice for Justice UK. (https://vfjuk.org.uk/vfjuk-supports-rse-report-challenging-government/).

[42] An individual doctor, when faced with a woman who requests an abortion, can exercise his or her right to conscientious objection, but must refer her to another doctor (see section 4 of the Abortion Act 1967). Conscientious objection cannot be exercised if it is necessary to save the woman's life or to prevent grave permanent injury to her physical or mental health.

[43] Abortion Statistics, England and Wales: 2018: Summary information from the abortion notification forms returned to the Chief Medical Officers of England and Wales (published 13 June 2019), Department of Health and Social Care, p. 12.

[44] https://www.who.int/classifications/icd/factsheet/en/

[45] Abortion Statistics, England and Wales: 2018, pp. 7-8 and 11.

[46] Ibid., p. 11.

[47] Ibid., p.18. In the Department of Health and Social Care's Summary information of abortion notification forms, it is unclear how many of these selective abortions involved embryos implanted through IVF.

[48] *Termination of Pregnancy for Fetal Abnormality in England, Scotland and Wales: Report of a Working Party*, Royal College of Obstetricians and Gynaecologists, May 2010, p.18. See: https://www.rcog.org.uk/globalassets/documents/guidelines/terminationpregnancyreport18may2010.pdf.

[49] Ibid. See Executive Summary and Recommendations.

[50] Ibid.

[51] *Parliamentary Inquiry into Abortion on the Grounds of Disability*, chaired by Fiona Bruce MP, July 2013, p. 4.

[52] For a full list of all the Commission's recommendations, see pp. 5-6.

[53] pp. 46-47.

[54] p. 49.

[55] https://www.parliament.uk/business/publications/written-questions-answers-statements/written-question/Lords/2016-03-17/HL7160/

Janet's Story

When I found out I was pregnant I was 35 years old. At that time, I had no income; I was in the country on a limited visa. Also, I was living with my brother; if he had discovered I was pregnant, he would have asked me to leave the house. Originally, the father of the child wanted me to become pregnant but then he changed his mind.

Given the circumstances, I felt I wasn't ready to bring a child into the world. I decided to book an appointment with my GP. I told the doctor I needed an abortion. An appointment was arranged for me at an abortion clinic in Richmond, south west London.

As I arrived at the clinic building, a lady engaged me in conversation. I told her about my situation and why I was seeking a termination. She gave me a leaflet and said that if I changed my mind, support would be offered to me.

I went into the abortion clinic, but as I sat in the waiting room, I decided to read the leaflet. It came from the Good Counsel Network (GCN). I realised then that if I could be offered the support I needed, I did want to keep my child. When it came to my turn, I was offered a consent form which would allow the medics to do the termination. I told them that if I could be offered support, I definitely would not be doing this. They told me they could not give me this support. They could only offer me the abortion.

After thinking about this, I thought about the support that was now being offered to me. With this help, I could have my child. It would work out for me. I told the clinic that I would need time to reconsider. Eventually, I chose to cancel the abortion and have my child.

Since I gave birth to my son, Felix, the father has registered himself as the child's father. But over the last few years, I have had no contact with him.

The people from the GCN have kept their promise. They provided me with accommodation. First, I was given somewhere to live for a few months until I gave birth. I remember thinking at the time that I had no worries or fears, because I would have a roof over my head. I was given breakfast, lunch and dinner. Once I had my baby boy, I was re-located to another address where the living conditions were more spacious for me and my child.

Eventually, social services provided me with a two-bedroom flat – but without furniture! I told Clare, who runs the GCN, about this problem and she arranged for a bed, sofa and washing machine to be brought across to the flat.

The people from GCN have also been helping me purchase baby clothes and food supplies. I have been helped with shopping and having Felix's clothes washed. They have been very helpful to me and my son.

Felix recently turned three years old.

Chapter Four

ABORTION IS A BIBLE ISSUE

Bishop Michael Nazir-Ali

The following chapter is the transcript of a talk given at the conference Slaughter of the Innocent *on 21 September 2019.*

This is not an apology for Bishops in the House of Lords, but you must know that when people do things there is a cost involved. I observed this in the House of Lords over many years. What is the cost in voting according to one's conscience on, for instance, the lowering of the age of consent, on same-sex relationships, on civil partnerships, on same-sex marriage, on abortion, on assisted dying or on freedom of thought and speech? The cost can be too high, and some people, very often good people, prefer to keep their heads down, seeking to escape extensive abuse and traducing in the media and elsewhere. I was a member of the HFEA (Human Fertilisation and Embryology Authority) and chair of its Ethics and Law Committee for six years, and when I was leaving the minister, who gives gongs to people as they leave, said to me, "Bishop, you have never been comfortable here, have you?" and I said, "No, I didn't come here to be comfortable." That is the point. You have to be prepared for discomfort if you are going to achieve anything. This is not going to happen in a safe way, with all your safety intact; sometimes even your sanity is at risk!

We have had some wonderful contributions today and I am so grateful that I have heard them all – a wonderful scientific and medical exposition from Professor Wyatt, together with many of the testimonies that have been so powerful, and I am grateful for them. I would just like to remind you of *why* we are pro-life, *why* we are pro-person, *why* we feel, as Christians, that God has made us in a certain way, and *why*, therefore, we should respect persons.

The Bible assumes that God begins His work in us and for us in the womb. Again and again the Bible tells us this. You will know all the more well-known examples: the example of Jeremiah, for instance, who was chosen from his mother's womb to carry out a ministry – actually quite an unpopular ministry, and perhaps we are called to be Jeremiahs today. (That's not a term of abuse; it's a good thing, to be a Jeremiah.) Then the Apostle Paul, though he came to the Christian faith late in the day, you might think, says in Galatians Chapter 1 that God had already chosen him before he was born from his mother's womb (verse 15). The writer of Psalm 139 is vividly aware of the intricacy of what goes on in the womb. Professor Wyatt was telling us how we now know what happens, but the Psalmist, when composing the Psalm, did not have the medical knowledge that we now have. Yet he was still able to say that God is already working in the womb as we are made, as we are created. Then there is Luke Chapter 1, which is actually cumulative: first the birth of John the Baptist is foretold (verses 8-20), then the birth of Jesus is foretold (verses 26-38), then comes the praise of Elizabeth (verses 42-45), and then the praise of Mary (verses 46-55).

To Mary, the angel says, "The Holy Spirit will come upon you, and the power of the Most High will overshadow you; therefore the child to be born will be called 'holy' – the Son of God." (verse 35, ESV). The story of Elizabeth and Mary is intimately connected with the nativity of Christ himself because, as we hear every advent as Christmas approaches, "In the sixth month the angel Gabriel was sent from God ... to a virgin ... [whose] name was Mary." (verses 26-27, ESV). We hear that again and again. The sixth month of what? Elizabeth's pregnancy. We don't know how long Mary's journey to the hill country may have been, but it would have been taken at an earlier stage of her pregnancy. We then find John the Baptist leaping in his mother's womb: you might think that that characterised the rest of his ministry, leaping about and telling people to repent; it clearly started very early! "And why is this granted to me that the mother of my Lord should come to me?" (verse 43, ESV), cries Elizabeth. Jesus has been in the womb for about three or four weeks. When Mary is called "the mother of God incarnate", "the mother of my Lord" or the "mother of the Lord Christ", that is not so much about Mary, it is about Jesus – who Jesus is. I think we should of course keep that in mind.

So the Biblical evidence is very strong, and the early Church is shown to be equally strong about the identity of what is in the womb. Again and again, in an early book of Christian instruction called the Didache, probably written around the same time as the New Testament, we find prohibition on abortion and on infanticide in the same sentence. That is also true of another very early document called the Letter of Barnabas (which is probably also first century); almost the same words are used. This suggests that these instructions are stylised, and that they were given to people being prepared for baptism in different settings. The early Church was known for rescuing mainly female children who had been exposed by their parents – that is to say, left to die. These parents did not have the guts to strangle them when they were born, so they left them in the streets, either to die or to be picked up by some generous person and brought up as their children. The early Church, particularly women, spent a lot of their time and money rescuing these children and making sure they had a good upbringing. For the early Church, abortion and infanticide were all of a piece. These early Christians did not make an arbitrary distinction between the unborn and the newly born. Now I say this because attempts are being made today to make that distinction, and from a Christian point of view that distinction is always illegitimate.

So why does the Bible, and why did the Church, regard abortion as unimaginable, as prohibited by God's law and purposes? I think it comes back to that basic teaching about the human person: that every human person has an inalienable dignity which cannot be taken away from them by other human beings because they are made in God's image. We do not determine who is made in God's image and who is not – this is a given for us, that we are made, that all human beings are made, in God's image. The only question that remains, therefore, is: when does a human person start to exist? If I may say so, we talk rather loosely about human life. My submission is that the question is not about human life. After all the human egg is human life and even human sperm is human life, but neither is a human person. So when does a human person come into being? That is the question.

Now in this I am bound to say that the Christian tradition has not always been as clear as it should have been, and one of the reasons for this is Exodus 21:22-24. This reads: "When men strive together, and hurt a woman with child, so that there is a miscarriage, and yet no harm follows, the one who hurt her shall be fined, according as the woman's husband shall lay upon him; and he shall pay as the judges determine. If any harm follows, then you shall give life for life, eye for eye, tooth for tooth ..." (RSV). The problem is this: the Greek translation of the Old Testament – the Septuagint – which was the Bible of the early Church, translates Exodus 21:22 to suggest that the miscarriage might be of what it calls an unformed foetus. Or it might be of a formed foetus. According to this translation, the passage prescribes different penalties, depending on whether the foetus is unformed or formed. So when a miscarriage occurs, caused by a fight between two men, and it leads to the death of an unformed foetus, a fine is imposed, but when the dead foetus is fully formed the harm calls for life for life, eye for eye, tooth for tooth. This meant that some of our great thinkers, like St Augustine of Hippo and St Jerome, taught that abortion would be homicide if the foetus were fully formed. It would be a grievous sin if the foetus were not fully formed, but it would not be homicide. This was reflected in the teaching of St Thomas Aquinas. It was based on the idea that I think Professor Wyatt was hinting at earlier, that in the early Church – and in early medicine as well – there was a particular time when the embryo or the foetus became 'ensouled'. I think 'quickened' was the term that was used. This kind of discussion persisted right down to the nineteenth century – for instance the Roman Catholic Church's definition that the human person begins at conception goes back to the clarifying of the Church's teaching in the nineteenth century, when much more was known medically and scientifically about what actually happens.

The question is, in the light of all this discussion, when is there a human person? Is there a human person at conception? All the genetic material that is needed for the human person is present at conception.

That is true, but then the objection is made that you can have twinning after conception and sometimes even tripling. So should we say, then, that at conception there is at least one person present? And possibly two or even three? And that there is never a case when there is no person present? Implantation is a very significant event in the life of the embryo and indeed the life of the mother. The development of brain activity and the nerve net, and the quickening, are all very significant events, so when is there a human person?

Now in the HFEA, where of course there is no agreement whatsoever on these issues, what I used to say was, "We don't need to agree in that context when there is a human person present." Because even if we don't know when exactly there is a human person, we should use the precautionary principle and always act as if there *is* a human person. I think the use of the precautionary principle is very widespread in science and I don't see why it is not more widely used in this area. That would give us very much the same kind of result, in public life, as insisting on the sanctity of the person from conception, which the Bible and Christian tradition compel us to do.

One of the things that is often said – I'm sure it's been said to you – is about the rights of the woman being based on autonomy. Autonomy is a big word in medicine – that everyone has the right to do with their body whatever they like. Now what I want to suggest is that autonomy is actually a distortion of the Christian idea of dignity – dignity in personhood. The Christian view, the Biblical view, of the person is that we become persons in relationship, whereas autonomy is about *individuals* in isolation. You see, you can't actually be a person in isolation. I am who I am because of my original interaction with my mother in the womb – how complex that interaction is. But then with my father, my siblings, with friends and of course with Christians in the Christian Church – that is what makes me a person. However, there are some things to be said about the plea that women make about the expectations held by society – expectations that society has of them, and of motherhood.

I think this is where the Church has to say something distinctive. I look forward to hearing what women have to say about this. But you can't have a proper exercise of motherhood if the models that you establish for work in society are all male, into which women are simply co-opted. I was reading an article in the press recently about breast-feeding. It said that a very high percentage of women in this country breast-feed for a few weeks after the birth of their child, and then the incidence of breast-feeding falls off dramatically. You don't need rocket science to work out why that is – it's because the mothers have to go back to work and can't continue to breast-feed. Unless we commend and work at models for women in productive employment, models that are not determined simply by men, we will have this issue raised again and again. Women have not been liberated. What has happened in the last century, generally speaking, is that they have been co-opted into a male world and made honorary men. Women will never be men because of their makeup – spiritually, physically, relationally, and in all sorts of ways. The challenge is, how do we produce a society which actually encourages women to be women, whether it's in work or in the family or in society generally?

Though much of our discussion, rightly of course, has been about abortion as it is traditionally understood, there is something else I want to say in this context: there is actually another danger, a very important issue, which is creeping up on us. And that is the wilful destruction of the embryo, either with fertility treatment or in the cause (allegedly) of scientific research. Many Christian women (and men) have IVF treatment to have a child, and I have been amazed how few have seen the moral issues attached to this. It is of course theoretically possible for a woman to produce in the course of her usual cycle a single egg, which can then be fertilised by the sperm of her husband *in vitro* and replanted into her, which may result in a pregnancy. But in fact that is not what happens with conventional IVF. The woman is stimulated to produce a number of eggs, which are then fertilised, either by the husband's sperm or somebody else's. Now, the HFEA allows only two fertilised eggs to be implanted at any one time. So what happens to the other embryos? They can be stored possibly for future use, although the storage is not permanent. Or they can be donated for research, which means they will have to be destroyed very quickly after their use; I think there is a fourteen-day limit. Or they can simply be 'disaggregated'. 'Disaggregated' means destroyed.

Pre-implantation genetic diagnosis was developed, so that embryos could be created and then inspected to see whether they had a heritable disease, like Thalassemia or Huntington's Chorea. If they had, they would not be implanted in the mother, but only the healthy embryos which were not carriers of the disease would be. Each case would come up for permission by the HFEA and its Ethics and Law Committee. So what do you do? In some cases it was clear that the embryo would not survive, or that any child that did manage to be born would not live very long or would not have a sustainable life. But the argument then came up, and this is a slippery slope, about non-heritable diseases – what do we do about them? There was a famous case where this line that had been drawn in the sand was moved, and so now in theory it is possible for Pre-implantation genetic diagnosis to be used for designer babies – babies that have the qualities you want them to have, and are free of susceptibility to disease and disability, which Robert Harris was talking about earlier.

So I would hope that when we talk about abortion, we look very seriously at the fertility industry, which is hugely lucrative and works on the systematic destruction of embryos for one reason or another, whether it's because experimentation on them is deemed essential for scientific progress, or because they're 'inconvenient' and unwanted, because of disability, or simply because they've been stored for what is deemed too long a period. These issues are 'invisible'. The kinds of abortion stories we have heard this morning are very visible and graphic – we praise God that people have made these decisions – but there is something unseen going on which is also morally wrong, and many people are complicit in this because of the desire to have a child. In many cases, IVF proves to be unnecessary because natural conception and birth is still possible, but people don't know that. They are bamboozled by the sales talk and are milked of resources, which they can sometimes ill afford, for a baby they might have had naturally anyway.

Finally, the question about support. I am glad that this morning the Good Counsel Network, and others who actually provide support for mothers who decide not to have an abortion, have been so prominently mentioned. I think this is hugely important. We cannot pontificate on this issue if we are not willing to have the facilities and resources that mothers need to bring up their children. If they can't bring them up then the possibility of fostering and adoption should always be there. I was troubled to learn that the number of babies being adopted continues to fall year on year. Has this anything to do with artificial reproduction techniques and their popularity? I'm quite sure that it does. More and more people, who might otherwise have adopted a baby, are now bending over backwards – financially and in terms of the demands on their bodies and their time – to have a child that is biologically their own, even if there are then 'spare' embryos, some of which are destroyed in the process. So we've got to step forward to help mothers bring up their children. It was such a scandal that the Catholic adoption agencies were closed down because they refused to compromise their position on adoption, that it should only be by a husband and wife. We do need to have arrangements for children to be adopted and looked after by people who care, if the mothers of these children, for whatever reason, cannot keep them.

Thank you very much indeed for what you have done this morning. I look forward to seeing how the work develops. One final point: it has been said here – and I think this is quite crucial – we need small groups of Christians in various localities who come together to pray and to work for the integrity of the human person as intended by God. This will apply of course to abortion, but also to assisted dying, and to many other moral questions that come up in hospitals and in homes. We need to uphold the person – as created by God and redeemed by the coming of Jesus and by His dying and rising. I know that Voice for Justice UK, Christian Concern and ParentPower all have databases. Don't just sit on them! Use them to create local groups that can make a change in their own communities.

Alina's Story

When I found out I was pregnant, I was worried because I was working as an au pair. I knew that if my boss discovered what was happening, I would be sacked and have nowhere to live. I knew I could not support the baby and myself financially.

I was feeling very conflicted about my options. If I went for an abortion, this would be against my beliefs and faith. I was brought up in the Romanian Orthodox Church and abortion is considered a sin.

I was not married at the time. Five weeks into my pregnancy, I told my boyfriend the news. (I had only found out I was pregnant at four weeks). He told me he didn't want the child and urged me to seek an abortion. He also explained that, financially, he wasn't able to provide support. However, I know this was not true, because his earnings were enough.

I decided not to tell my family about my dilemma. They believe that sex outside marriage is wrong. At this point, I felt I had messed up my life. What was I to do?

I spoke to some of my friends, asking them what I should do. They all felt that I should go for an abortion. If I didn't have the financial support, then how could I have a child? Part of me was persuaded by what they said. Another part of me felt this was not the right decision. I really didn't want to abort my child. It didn't feel right.

When I phoned the Marie Stopes abortion clinic in London, I was eight weeks into my pregnancy. Although they were a charity, they were unable to provide the help I needed. When speaking to one of their staff, I said that I was looking for help and support to have my baby, but the woman told me that the only help they could provide was giving me an abortion.

On my way to the clinic for my appointment, I cried all the time. I also prayed to God asking him to show me a sign. If only there was a way to stop this! I wanted to find a way out of this course which I was about to take.

As I approached the clinic, I was offered a leaflet by a lady outside the building. She was from an organisation called the Good Counsel Network (GCN). She had a conversation with me. I told her that I didn't want an abortion, but I had no financial support, so how could I have a child? She assured me that any material support I required would be provided, including housing, if I chose to have my child. I struggled to believe this. Not even friends would offer this kind of support, so why would complete strangers?

When I spoke to a woman inside the clinic, she said, "They are deceiving you." She was referring to the people I had spoken to outside the clinic. I said I didn't want an abortion but only support, so that I could have my child. In response, the woman told me, "We only offer abortion."

Two days later, I had another appointment at the clinic. As I walked into the building, I saw all these women waiting around for their appointments. Their faces looked so sad. It was a horrible sight. I went in to see someone. She told me, "You have to be selfish. You have to move on." I was thinking to myself, "If I just have the abortion, I can, as this woman was saying, just get on with my life." But I felt very conflicted. How could I kill my child? I reminded myself that abortion is wrong.

As I sat in office talking to this woman, my phone rang. It was a lady from the GCN. Within seconds of talking to her, I felt I had to have my baby. My decision was now made. I immediately got up from my seat and left.

I eventually had my baby, a daughter. I am so happy I chose life for my child. It could so easily have gone the other way, and she would now not be alive. She would not exist.

What is remarkable is that when I was aged 11, I remember having a dream. In this dream, I was an adult woman who was walking with her child through some fields. This child was a mixed-race girl. What is so remarkable and prophetic is that not only is my daughter mixed-race, but also that she looks exactly like the girl in the dream!

But my story doesn't end there, because I got pregnant again a few years later. On this occasion, the doctors gave me a diagnosis that was enough to worry any mother. They said the child would have a serious disability and would not live for long. The doctors told me I should abort. They were very insistent. It felt as though I had no option but to agree to what they were saying.

I thought and prayed long and hard about this. It was not easy. I decided I was going to have this child, no matter what the outcome. On the day of my labour, I gave birth to a baby boy. Tragically, he lived for only 3 hours. This was very traumatic. But I believe I did the right thing. My boy was given a name. I had a birth certificate issued for him. This showed that he was treated as a human being like everyone else who had entered this world. I also made sure he was given a burial. I know I did the right thing in allowing him to come into the world, though it was against the advice of the doctors. The burial also brought an important closure to the short chapter of my son's life – he had the right to be treated as any other human being who is born. And the closure helped me too.

When I talk with my friends now – the ones who had urged me to abort my daughter – they are so happy for me. However, some say to me, with sadness, that if they had not had their abortions, their children would be a certain age now. They regret their decision. A couple of these friends are now unable to have their own children because of infertility. They feel great regret that, when they could conceive, they chose instead to abort their baby. Now it is too late for them. I feel so sorry for them.

As regards my own decisions, I am very glad I chose to have my daughter. She is so precious. But, were it not for the financial help the GCN have provided me with, all along, I am sure I would have aborted her. It is not easy to say this. However, I felt my options at the time were very limited. I am so thankful for the help I have received from this group over the years.

Chapter Five

ABORTION – A WINNABLE BATTLE

Andrew Stephenson

Our aversion to handling difficult subjects, for reasons such as self-preservation, has resulted in two things: passivity in the face of injustice, and the hijacking of the narrative by those with a deadly agenda.

It is no wonder, then, that the situation for the unborn child has worsened, when for years we have agreed to engage in dialogue within the rules of engagement set by the pro-abortion lobby. In the absence of robust challenge, this lobby has re-framed the debate to a more palatable discourse, numbing much of the general public to the true horror of abortion. It is hard to demonstrate what abortion is and what it does when you are confined to discursive terms such as 'reproductive freedom', 'choice' and 'equal rights'.

Merely talking about abortion is not enough.

I became aware of this issue at a time when it appeared that the UK offered only two answers to the problem of unplanned pregnancy. The most common was pastoral work (which is certainly necessary); the other, a direct appeal to MPs through letter-writing. Neither met the issue head on. They are essential, and we need more of both, but without addressing the misconceptions, little is going to change.

Reality tells a different story. For instance, if women did not believe their baby was really a baby, then why would they go to a Crisis Pregnancy Centre, which could help them *through* 'their problem', rather than to an abortion clinic which was offering to '*get rid of their problem*'? The unpalatable truth is that MPs will not propose pro-life legislation, if the loudest voice they hear is from rambunctious lobbyists stigmatising the backward idea of wanting to protect babies.

Until recently, the pro-life movement, globally, had not adopted the purpose of changing public opinion. A significant portion of its efforts consisted of unevidenced assertions about 'morality'. But merely expressing opposition to abortion, while this can make us feel better about the problem, does nothing to communicate the reasons why it is 'bad'.

If we accept the pro-choice narrative, it only feeds into the agenda of women's rights – and hiding the reality of injustice is part of this agenda.

The insight that 'a picture paints a thousand words' is not a recent discovery, so why do pro-lifers still rely so heavily on employing the written or spoken word alone? Holding up a placard with the words 'Abortion is murder', in a post-modern, post-literate culture, does little to convince the culture that the claim is true. "That's just your opinion", thinks the viewer, before dismissing the message.

I realised early on that the over-riding themes of pro-life conferences did not grapple with the enormity of what we were up against. You would think that, at best, all we could do was to maintain the status quo; at worst, we would have to concede some ground because the problem of abortion was too entrenched to fight. Most pro-lifers, I knew, had given up all reasonable hope of ever seeing the tide turn.

The work of the Center for Bio-Ethical Reform (CBR) caught and held my attention because it was strategy-based, as opposed to focusing merely on tactics. Through the application of that strategy, many were shifting their opinion towards an informed and life-affirming position. I was impressed that the simplicity of the strategy's application meant that ordinary men and women could achieve extraordinary results.

The Centre for Bio-Ethical Reform UK is affiliated with CBR, which operates around the world. Like CBR it bases its strategy on a detailed analysis of the history of social reform, and then applies the principles of successful reform movements to the abortion battle. The patterns that are emerging, the same as those in past movements, indicate that this is very much a winnable battle. These principles for social reform are so critical that, if ignored, evil will freely prevail. But when put into practice, these essential ingredients will erode the foundations, the justifications and the lifespan of that evil.

The better-known aspect of our work involves displaying large banners showing the victims of abortion. Of course, this is unpleasant to see, but it cannot be more unpleasant than the act of abortion itself. The key principle is to do with visibility: injustice that is invisible will inevitably be tolerated, but injustice that is exposed will inevitably become intolerable. Unless we settle the facts about who the baby is, and what abortion does to that baby, we will only serve the idea that abortion is a morally inconsequential act, rather than an act of violence that kills a baby – thought of as wrong, perhaps, but the lesser of two evils.

Not everyone is comfortable with CBR's strategy, and people will often say, "There must be a better way". Looking for a better way is fine – so long as we mean better for the cause, not better for our popularity.

We have bought into the lie that, in order to be effective, we must be liked. Thank God that William Wilberforce, whose image was burnt in effigy by his contemporaries,[1] did not rely on this indicator of success. CBR's founder, Gregg Cunningham, has said, "Effective reformers are seldom liked, and liked reformers are seldom effective." In fact, some of the most effective reformers in the past have been killed for their cause.

The media have dutifully mischaracterised our projects, our staff and our volunteers, which has contributed to the negative response to our work. On the upside, however, media attention has allowed our imagery to be seen by a much wider audience than we could have managed on our own.

For over fifty years many in the pro-life movement have in fact covered up the horror of abortion, working just as hard as those in the abortion lobby who are doing the same thing! But we pro-lifers then scratch our heads, wondering why no one seems bothered by the horror. Society needs to be awakened to its blind spot. The truth must be revealed; exposing the deeds of darkness should only be avoided if we are looking to make friends.

When pro-lifers do use images, they tend to use pictures of born babies. These photos could be useful if a large portion of the nation believed that killing new-born babies was a good idea. As a colleague has noted, however, if one of the largest abortion providers in the UK feels safe using born-baby images, then we should realise that cutesy baby photos will make no difference at all to the way people view early abortion.

The historian and author, Adam Hochschild, makes this remark about the abolitionists, at the close of his book *Bury The Chains – The British Struggle to Abolish Slavery*:

> *They believed that because human beings had a capacity to care about the suffering of others, exposing the truth would move people to action. "We are clearly of opinion," Granville Sharp wrote to a friend later that year, "that the nature of the slave-trade needs only to be known to be detested." Clarkson, writing of this "enormous evil" said that he "was sure that it was only necessary for the inhabitants of this favoured island to know it, to feel a just indignation against it." It was this faith that led him to buy handcuffs, shackles, and thumbscrews to display to the people he met on his travels.[2]*

We need to help members of the public feel an affinity with a victim, so that their hearts are stirred out of apathy. Images have the power to expose euphemisms and radically change the way we feel about an issue. Changed feelings are more likely to lead to changed thinking which, we hope, will also change how we behave. Changed thinking must precede changed behaviour.

Videos on our social media of members of the public moving from a 'pro-choice' to a 'pro-life' stance represent the tip of the iceberg. The public mood is shifting rapidly on this issue.

The strategy is effective, and it is gaining momentum. Enquirers are signing up at a rate that our current infrastructure and resources are struggling to cope with.

What is the result?

I have lost count of the times we have been told, "If I had seen the abortion pictures I would never have had an abortion." There is an increase in righteous anger towards the system that has caused this immense pain in the lives of families.

It has been a privilege to receive photographs from parents who have changed their minds about having an abortion, after seeing pictures of its reality. We much prefer their pictures to ours, of course, but it is indisputable that, without the horrific pictures, the beautiful ones would not exist. Those very same children could have ended up looking like the images on our banners, if our work was not guided by the conviction about what needs to be done. A baby's first photo should never be one that captured their death.

Ultimately, our goal is not simply to save lives by ones and twos, but peacefully to bring down the machinery that allows abortion to happen.

Here are two principles that we can apply for the abolition of abortion:

1) To change public policy effectively, we must change public opinion.

Grassroots movements need to create an appetite for reform. The pro-abortion lobby has already done this by talking about 'choice'. We must shift the message to focus on what it is that is being chosen.

2) No social reformer has ever ended an injustice by covering it up.

Every successful social reform movement has required activists to 'make real' the humanity of the victims and the inhumanity of those who oppress them. The Transatlantic slave trade abolitionists did this very effectively by using iconic images, such as Josiah Wedgwood's kneeling slave with the caption, "Am I not a man and a brother?" Thomas Clarkson's diagram of the slave ship *Brookes* was a powerful tool for conveying the brutal conditions of the passage across the Atlantic. More powerful still, visually, were William Blake's etchings, depicting the sheer bloody violence faced by any slave who crossed the very thin line between acceptable and unacceptable behaviour towards his or her master.

The cover-up we live with today contributes to the lie that abortion is merely 'the removal of a pregnancy using gentle suction', as the providers cruelly describe it.

Hiding the truth allows the pro-abortion lobby to deceive the public about the magnitude of the horror of abortion.

As for the reformers, rather than stating the conclusion about abortion that they hope the public will arrive at, it is their role to provide the best evidence, evidence that will compel the public to take hold of that very conclusion.

A large portion of the population knows that there is something wrong about abortion, but usually they greatly underestimate just how bad it is. We have plenty of video evidence of members of the public telling us that they have changed their minds about abortion, once they have seen for themselves what is involved. The comment, "I know what abortion is, I just didn't know it was like THAT!", is not infrequently heard on our educational displays.

When the perpetrators of abortion are allowed to dominate the narrative, they will always paint themselves favourably, and describe their opponents with vitriol. The reality of abortion is hidden behind euphemisms, but allowing that to continue unabated is to allow the killing of babies that could have been saved. Proponents of abortion will not talk about killing babies, of course; they prefer to talk about reproductive health. They won't talk about a baby but a pregnancy; they refer not to an abortionist but to a healthcare provider.

Transatlantic slave trade abolitionists were up against the same problem. The term 'slave-owner' was avoided – it sounded malevolent – and other titles – planters, proprietors, merchants or country gentlemen – were preferred. Such a phenomenon of denial would lead the most narcissistic of the guilty, when challenged, to claim to be the victim.

Our images and footage accurately contrast what the unborn child looks like, on the way into an abortion clinic, with his or her appearance on leaving. Search any abortion provider's website and literature, and the information that we are showing is precisely the information that the providers deliberately and cruelly leave out. This deception is justified, arrogantly, on the grounds that all women know exactly what they are going to do. But in effect, when we stand outside a clinic with our banners, it is as though we are removing the walls for the world to see what is going on inside.

Far from being an unwinnable battle, abortion could soon be a thing of the past; the keys to victory are already available, and we could end this evil within the next five years.

The sheer horror of the facts is sufficient for the practice to collapse under its own weight. Attempts to introduce buffer zones, under the guise of 'protecting women', only safeguard women from the facts that the providers deliberately withhold; the equivalent of forced abortion.[3]

It is clear that public opinion is indeed changing, when people are faced with the facts about abortion. Millions of women, who were manipulated into thinking that abortion was the right option for them, are now suffering the physical and psychological consequences of abortion. How then should we expect them to respond when they discover that those who caused their pain were driven by ideology and the desire for profit?

The Nuremberg Tribunal determined abortion to be a crime against humanity within the legal definition of murder.[4] The International Criminal Court Act 2001 adopts this definition into domestic law. No serious pro-lifer would hold that international law incriminates women who have abortions, but it does incriminate the architects of mass destruction who adopt policies which are themselves criminal.[5]

It is easy to be a hindsight hero, but not so simple to confront an injustice when it is at our door. We need to make the decision now as to how historians and society will judge our actions, or lack thereof.

If you would like to support the work of the Centre for Bio-Ethical Reform UK, please get in touch on info@cbruk.org.

Endnotes

---

[1] Hochschild, A, *Bury The Chains – The British Struggle to Abolish Slavery,* (1st edition) (Mariner Books, New York, 2005), p.124.

[2] Hochschild, op. cit., p.366.

[3] Article 39 of the Council of Europe Convention on preventing and combating violence against women and domestic violence (Istanbul, 11.V.2011) defines forced abortion as 'performing an abortion on a woman without her prior and informed consent' and requires its criminalisation. It is submitted that the application of any pressure at all for a woman to undergo an abortion suffices to establish it as a forced abortion.

[4] Tuomala, JC, *Nuremberg and the Crime of Abortion*, 42 U. Toledo. L. Rev. 283, https://digitalcommons.liberty.edu/cgi/viewcontent.cgi?article=1047&context =lusol_fac_pubs

[5] Section 4 of the Abortion Act 1967 and section 38 of the Human Fertilisation and Embryology Act 1990 make provision for conscientious objection to participation in abortion and in the making, keeping, use and destruction of human embryos. In 2010, the Parliamentary Assembly of the Council of Europe adopted Resolution 1763 (2010) which reads: *"No person, hospital or institution shall be coerced, held liable or discriminated against in any manner because of a refusal to perform, accommodate, assist or submit to an abortion, the performance of a human miscarriage, or euthanasia or any act which could cause the death of a human foetus or embryo, for any reason."*

The judgement of the conscientious objector that these wilful acts amount to the murder, extermination and inhumane treatment of innocent human beings must be regarded in law as correct for the internal forum, and as conclusive to determine the construction of the terms identifying the conduct elements of crimes against humanity. The judgement of the Nuremberg Military Tribunal, in the case of *United States v Greifelt & Others* [1948], that abortion was correctly indicted as a crime within its jurisdiction, presupposes that it is in international law murder and – when committed as part of a mass killing event – extermination. This is confirmed by the Second Recital in the Preamble to the Rome Statute of the International Criminal Court 1998: *"Mindful that during this century millions of children, women and men have been victims of unimaginable atrocities that deeply shock the conscience of humanity."*

The International Criminal Court Act 2001 gives domestic legal effect to the Rome Statute for the period commencing 1 January 1991.

Chapter Six

CRISIS PREGNANCY
– OFFERING REAL CHOICE

Clare McCullough

We never know the fullness of the plans God has for us, even when they are right around the corner. I was certainly oblivious to where He would take me when I started thinking about getting involved in pro-life work.

Personally, I would have chosen political campaigning against abortion. This was the work I had most supported, growing up in a Catholic family which was very pro-life.

I thought caring for women who were vulnerable to abortion was something important, but I supposed it was happening already and that I would not be very good at it anyway. I had no experience of pregnancy, babies, crisis pregnancy situations or anything else that was relevant.

I also felt that political campaigning was likely to make a much more direct impact on abortion laws. And I really did want to see major changes in the abortion law, which was allowing the best part of 200,000 babies to die each year in England and Wales.

I had just finished University and an aunt of mine, passing through London, decided to take me to Dublin as a graduation present! I went gladly. On my check list of things to do was to stop off and visit some pro-life groups I admired. When I reached one office, to my dismay I found that everyone had set off on their summer tour of the country, and would not be back during my short stay. I headed back to my accommodation, but on the way bumped into another group, which had just been formed; these people were offering real alternatives to women trapped in difficult circumstances in pregnancy.

I listened with interest to the accounts of what they were doing. What struck me most was that their work was aimed at women who were set on abortion. They had discovered that many women who were set on abortion felt that way because a) they were in impossible situations, b) they were under tremendous pressure from others, and c) they had no good alternatives to the abortion decision as far as they could see. The next thing that struck me was that the work of this group was totally founded on their faith. And yet they were helping women of all faiths and no faith, with no proselytizing. Many women did come to have a faith in God, or returned to an abandoned or weak faith with a new vigour, but this was because of the support and the witness they had received, not because of coercion, or because there were strings attached. Knowing little about the 'care' side of pro-life work, I was shocked to discover that many, many women did not even know that help was available to them in their crisis pregnancy situations; they certainly didn't know how to find it. Many women who considered themselves pro-life were in fact having abortions because they thought they had no alternative.

I regret to say that I did not rush back to London to start this work, but rather dithered about, thinking about this work with great admiration but with a total lack of commitment. God was not so indecisive, however, and He used the next year or two to form me for this work by involving me in apostolates, which taught me to serve Christ in others. However, a day came when I got a phone call from the people I had met in Ireland, asking me to get involved in starting a similar centre in the UK. Under their guidance, and with the help of others, I did so.

From the day The Good Counsel Network (GCN) (www.goodcounselnetwork.com) started work in London, on the 13th January 1997, we realised that God was at work in our centre. We tried to co-operate with Him and not put obstacles in His way. In fact, we were always putting obstacles in His way, through our weakness, desire for human respect and so on, but despite this He responded to our willingness to try! I soon learnt that if we really listened to the women we met with, and helped them to build their own solutions, most women changed their minds about abortion. For most women abortion is the last option, but one that quickly becomes the only option if partner, family and circumstances do not have real support to offer. When the woman designs her own solution, the GCN steps in to try to help her build that solution. Financial help, practical help, friendship and moral support combine to do for each woman the very best we can. Additionally, we pray for every woman we see, for the decision she is about to make, for her baby, for the wellbeing of both of them, for her loved ones, and for the future.

Success came quickly. The first woman I met with was in her forties. She had an older child, a problem with substance addiction, and a broken history. I was so out of my depth. But I felt that if there was anything in this work that was true, it was that our good God hates abortion, but that He loves, and sent His Son to die for, the women we were meeting, and their children too. Therefore, if we trusted Him, He was going to provide for them. Confidence in Him, as well as absolute determination to be like good family to these women, were our winning strategies! That first lady changed her mind and kept her baby. We provided the support we had promised and she rejoiced that she was able to avoid the abortion she did not want.

Over the next 20 years women kept coming. Some would be tearful, some angry, some dead set on abortion, most very hurt by those who had let them down. All kinds of women changed their minds about abortion. When there is real support, and companionship, women are capable of much heroism. But we also saw that these women's lives improved in many ways, despite the practical difficulties of having an "unplanned" child.

Typically, women would say "I love my baby so much, I had no idea I could love her this much. She is the joy of my life." And often those who had most pressured her to abort (usually her boyfriend, husband or parents) would be around when the baby was born, wanting to be involved. But when this didn't happen, because they abandoned her, we stepped in as her adopted extended family.

To give some examples, Rebecca came from a family that had suffered horrendous abuse and they had been subjected to much brutality. Rebecca herself was in an abusive relationship – the abuse was going both ways, by her own admission. She worked out that between them the women in her family had been through about 16 abortions. She herself had had 4. She met a pavement counsellor from the GCN outside an abortion centre, where we were giving out leaflets with information about how to get help. (These leaflets give information on the development of the baby, the risks of abortion, and the financial, practical and moral support that we offer.) On meeting the counsellor, Rebecca burst into tears and said she needed to talk to someone other than the abortion centre staff, so she came to our centre again and again and again, just to talk. Not only did she keep her baby, but also this had a huge impact on her family, causing many of them to think again about abortion and to change their views, when they saw the beautiful, much loved child she bore. We gave her a little financial support and some baby goods, and we helped her argue her case for new housing with her council. Such a great reward for such a little work on our part!

Annette was a mother who found us through a friend. She was one of many expectant mothers we have helped who were victims of rape. Annette was raped by an employer and lost her job, as well as becoming pregnant after the rape. She had many problems because of this, financial and housing being two of them. She also had a husband living abroad, to whom she planned to return, and they had older children already grown up. Her biggest problem, though, was the fact that the baby had been conceived in rape. Surprising as it may seem, of the women who have become pregnant through rape and who have come to our centre, over 50 per cent have wanted to keep their baby. And indeed, the largest study of rape victims who became pregnant, found the same thing. It is true that many do experience feelings of repulsion on discovering that they are pregnant, and some initially reject the baby, seeing it as a 'monster' because of how conception occurred. But, as the baby grows, the mother often begins to recognise the child as *her* child rather than the rapist's child, and sometimes she will identify with the child, seeing both herself and the child as victims of the rapist – as they are, in fact. Sometimes women have strong feelings – or even strong moral values – about not wanting to have an abortion, and the fact that she has been raped does not necessarily make her want to go against these values or gut instincts.

Like many other women in this position, Annette chose to give her baby life. We provided support but she made her own decision, with our moral support, to allow her baby to grow and then to give him up for adoption. The police told her they would not prosecute the rapist if she kept the baby – this may not actually have been police policy, and they did eventually take the rapist to court, but this is what was said to her – but she kept her child anyway. She said she would give him up for adoption when he was born. When he was born, Annette went to an adoption agency and signed her child away. (He was still in hospital at this point.) Immediately after leaving their office, Annette was struck with a strong sense that it was a huge mistake. She ran back to the agency, which was closed by then, and sat on the step sobbing. Early the next morning she went back there and tore up the papers. She phoned her husband and, when he got over the shock of all that had happened, he agreed to accept – and love – the child.

In total there have been about three thousand two hundred women who have come to us in person – there have been many more, of course, who have contacted us over the phone or online. For these women – feeling unsure about what to do, or set on the idea of abortion – the support we offer has changed everything. This support has included:

- showing them their baby on a scan (we can obtain a private scan)

- explaining their rights to maternity benefits

- assuring them that we will help them keep a roof over their head, or provide one if all else fails

- introducing them (or, where this is inconvenient, connecting them by phone) to others from similar situations, who also got help to keep their baby

- putting them in touch with someone else whose baby had a similar serious or life-limiting condition

- helping them escape an abusive situation

- providing good legal advice about their immigration status

- offering real friendship

When practical help is offered, and received, it allows the woman to have the freedom to choose life.

Of course, there are others: the women who did not choose life, those for whom information about their developing baby, financial help, practical help, moral support, prayer and encouragement, simply were not enough to change their minds. We regard these women as our sisters. Many of them suffer immensely in making this decision, and afterwards. We are still there for them. We are still praying for them. Some come back in a future pregnancy, seeking our help, and these women are met with great joy! We pray for the day when no woman will ever have to consider abortion as an option, when abortion will not exist as an option! But today, while abortion remains legal, and doctors and advisers tell women 'It's for the best', 'It's not really a baby yet', or 'Abortion is healthcare', we pray for those who, under pressure and often at the most difficult moment in their lives, choose abortion.

From 2011 to the present, the main bulk of our work has been offering alternatives to women outside abortion centres. Our vigils consist of a small number of praying people (often one or two) a few metres from the abortion centre and one person offering a help leaflet at the abortion centre gate. The aim is to witness peacefully against abortion a little distance away, and to offer real help and alternatives to women on the doorstep of the abortion centre. We pray for the women, their partners and the children, for the abortion centre staff and for all involved. We judge nobody, but we are there to assist those women who want to avoid abortion to find an escape route, and to offer hope and healing to those who are distressed after having an abortion. We have held regular daily vigils at three London abortion centres: Marie Stopes in central London, Marie Stopes in Ealing, and British Pregnancy Advisory Service (BPAS) in Twickenham. The last two of these centres are two of the busiest abortion centres in the country. Over the years when we have been praying and offering help outside these centres, we have seen well over 1,000 women choose life for their children – more than 500 in Ealing alone.

It should hardly be surprising then – since abortion provides a lucrative income – that when a local group of young women who describe themselves as 'pro-choice' formed to protest against the

'Religious Vigils', Marie Stopes and BPAS immediately backed their campaign. BPAS set up a well-funded Back Off campaign, which sought to build a narrative of abuse and harassment outside the abortion centres, and to demand the imposition of buffer zones. A buffer zone would prevent us from reaching out to any woman entering an abortion centre. Their highly successful campaign worked by ignoring the testimonies of women who had welcomed and received our help, and by building up a store of alleged testimonies from women who claimed to have been harassed and abused by our vigils. The complete absence of CCTV footage of any of this alleged harassment, despite every abortion centre having CCTV, was ignored. Also ignored was the fact that many testimonies of harassment did not fit with the times, dates or circumstances of the vigils. In addition, many of those submitting such testimonies objected to any pro-life presence at all, and considered one person handing out a leaflet to be 'harassment'. The first Buffer Zone in Ealing was established in April 2018, followed by a second one in Richmond in 2019. In September 2018, the then Home Secretary, Sajid Javid, at the end of a review on abortion clinic protests, decided that it was not a 'proportionate' response to introduce national buffer zones. He said that 'what is clear from the evidence we gathered is that ... predominantly, anti-abortion activities are ... passive in nature.'[1] It is worth noting that individuals choosing to be part of our vigils agree to act peacefully, respectfully and within the law, and volunteers are asked to sign a 'Statement of Peace'.[2] We are committed to ensuring that our volunteers conduct themselves peacefully in all situations.

One brave mother whom we assisted through our vigils, who went on herself to offer help to many other women, is now fighting these buffer zones through the courts. Meanwhile, BPAS and others continue to fight for more buffer zones in London, Manchester and across the UK.

I said that before starting this work, 'I felt that political campaigning was likely to make a much more direct impact on abortion laws'. I now feel that, while a variety of works are needed to end abortion, the work of caring for these mothers is in fact the most important work we can do. It underpins all other pro-life work, for how can we change laws or even teach the truth about abortion if we offer these women no help? Even if abortion were no longer the normal 'solution' that many women opt for, the offer of practical help would remain a necessity. Put differently, it is one thing when we merely say that abortion is wrong, but when we offer concrete practical solutions and support to women, the whole situation changes, and often the woman's whole life changes for the better.

As it says in the Bible, James 2:15-16, *Suppose a brother or a sister is without clothes and daily food. If one of you says to them, 'Go in peace; keep warm and well fed,' but does nothing about their physical needs, what good is it?* (NIVUK)

I have also seen that the one-to one outreach to thousands of women with an uncompromising message of respect for the sanctity of human life – combined with the message that 'You and your children are not disposable', and backed with prayer and concrete help – is both winning and life-transforming. It changes hearts and minds, it changes the hearts and minds of whole families and communities.

Therefore, let me finish with the words of one of the mothers we have been privileged to serve. Explaining to members of Richmond Council why she disagreed with the Buffer Zone they had introduced, she said:

"Honestly, you cannot receive that kind of support anywhere else. If the people from GCN can't stand by the gate, it means you put vulnerable women, mothers, human beings, in danger. ... These pro-life people need to be standing there outside the abortion clinics. I have never received such support – when you go to some places, they say; we are here for you, we are here to support you, they always start like that. But everything is just on paper or it's just what they say. ... But here with GCN it's not like you have your baby and you are on your own after that – this is very important. They are there from the beginning until you are ready to stand on your own two feet – what is wrong with that? I really believe if I had met them years ago, my life would have been different." *Ilda, a mother assisted by The Good Counsel Network, giving testimony to Richmond Council in 2019.*

Endnotes

---

1 https://www.parliament.uk/business/publications/written-questions-answers-statements/written-statement/Commons/2018-09-13/HCWS958/

2 https://www.goodcounselnet.co.uk/Statement-of-Peace.html

Avelina's Story

A few years ago, I arrived in the UK from India with my husband and two boys, aged 5 and 13. Months later, I found myself pregnant and felt very disturbed. My husband and I were not ready for another child, certainly not financially. I was not mentally prepared for a third child.

I felt distressed because I was in a country that was new to me, but when someone suggested I have an abortion, I was thrown into turmoil. As a Catholic, I knew it was wrong to abort a baby, so I prayed to God. I didn't know what else to do. I felt so pressured, and my husband wanted me to have the abortion. My life became very hard.

When I eventually went to the abortion clinic, I saw that there were people praying outside. I discovered they were from the Good Counsel Network (GCN). As I approached the building, one woman offered me a leaflet. I took it. When I entered the building, they told me that if I had come for an abortion, I must throw away the leaflet I was holding in my hand. I was also informed that I had to book an appointment online, and I would need to take medication. A woman handed me another leaflet, then, without asking, took the leaflet I had been given earlier, out of my hand.

On my second visit to the same clinic, I noticed many people outside the building praying with the rosary, some bearing a Mother Mary image. I was feeling guilty; I knew I didn't really want an abortion. But one of the workers from the clinic, who happened to be passing, told me not to look at the people outside, and to enter the clinic by another door. I felt so guilty. I knew what I was about to do was a sin and it was not good for me.

I was offered another leaflet by the people outside, and I took it, and then entered the building through another entrance. Later that day, after returning home and thinking about what was happening, I called the GCN Helpline and spoke to Clare, the lady in charge. I told her about my situation and she understood, and told me she would do her best to help me.

She connected me with another woman, Andrea, who talked to me. I told her how disturbed I was feeling, and the situation I was facing. From that moment, she and another woman from the organisation became my friends.

They offered me the financial support I needed, so I decided I would go ahead and have my child. My baby was delivered on 20th June 2019. His name is Juan.

It always felt impossible for me to bring another child into the world because of the circumstances my husband and I found ourselves in, but these people helped me. They supported us and became my friends.

If a leaflet had not been given to me, I would have lost my beautiful child.

Glossary

Abortion

The deliberate ending of a pregnancy so that it does not result in the birth of a live child. Abortions may either be medical or surgical.

Medical abortions are of two kinds: taking an abortion pill to bring about a miscarriage (up to 10 weeks' gestation). This is known as early medical abortion. A pill is also taken for abortions between 10 and 24 weeks' gestation.

Surgical abortions take one of two forms. Up to 15 weeks' gestation, the foetus is removed by means of suction; this is known as vacuum aspiration. Between 15 and 24 weeks' gestation, the foetus is removed by the use of narrow forceps and suction; this is known as dilation and evacuation.

Embryo

The developing baby from the time of fertilisation up to the end of the seventh week.

Foetus (or Fetus)

From the eighth week, the developing baby is called a foetus.

Gestation

The period of development within which the unborn child is inside the mother's womb.

Gynaecology

A discipline within medicine that deals with the treatment of medical conditions and diseases of the female reproductive system.

Miscarriage

When a baby is prematurely and spontaneously expelled from the womb and dies. Unlike an abortion, a miscarriage is unintentional and therefore not the result of any deliberate act to end the pregnancy.

Morning after pill

This is also known as emergency contraception. The fertilised egg, which has yet to settle in the lining of the womb (implantation), is aborted by means of a pill. Depending on which pill is taken, the result is achieved within a period of up to five days. Legally, this is not treated as an abortion. Likewise, the official medical consensus does not categorise this as abortion. However, the outcome is abortifacient.

Neonatology

The branch of medicine that deals with the care, development, and diseases of new-born infants up to 28 days after birth.

Obstetrics

The branch of medicine that deals with the care given to women before, during and after pregnancy.

Pro-Choice

The belief or stance that affirms a woman's 'right to choose' whether she carries her baby to term or aborts it. The unborn child is not considered as having an inherent right to life. It is the woman, not the child, who holds rights.

Pro-Life

The belief or stance that affirms the unborn child's inherent right to life and to be born, resting on the principle of the sanctity of life. There are some limited circumstances under which some pro-lifers may accept abortion, for example, when a mother's life is at risk.

Termination

Another word for abortion.

Viability

The capacity of the foetus to survive independent of the mother. While the legal age of viability in the UK is 24 weeks' gestation, increasing numbers of premature children born under 24 weeks are surviving, on account of advancing medical support.

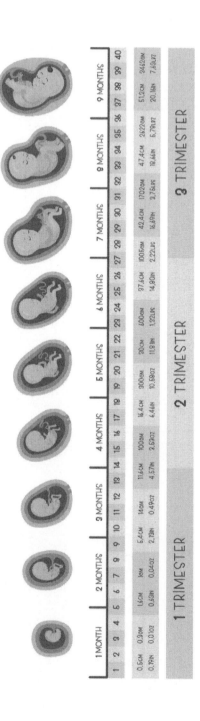

Timeline of Embryo and Foetal Development in the Womb

There are two methods of measuring gestational age: one based on the date of the last menstrual period, the other based on the date of conception.

First Trimester

1-3 weeks

The nucleus of male and female gametes (sperm and egg cells) fuse together (fertilisation) and penetrates into the womb lining (implantation).

In each gamete, there are 23 chromosomes. At fertilisation, the combined numbers of chromosomes from the male (father) and female (mother) gametes makes 46 in total.

The resulting cell (zygote) contains two sets of chromosomes, from the sperm and egg cells respectively. In other words, half of the DNA is from the father and half from the mother. DNA is the material inside the nucleus of the cells that carries all the genetic information of a human being.

The zygote undergoes cell division to become an embryo, reproducing identical cells.

As the cells begin to differentiate, they become more specialised in function. When the embryo is made up of eight cells, most of these embryonic cells begin to take on specialist roles, known as differentiation (e.g. the brain and spinal column, etc, will begin forming at three weeks).

Eyes begin to form; brain, spinal column, and nervous system are almost complete.

At 24 days, the heart begins to beat.[1]

4 weeks[2]

Muscles are developing; arm and leg buds become visible. Blood flows in the baby's veins; this is separate from the mother's blood.

5 weeks[3]

The baby's pituitary gland is forming; the mouth, ears, and nose are taking shape.

6 weeks

The baby's cartilage skeleton is completely formed.[4] Bone formation begins. The heart begins to beat.[5] There is the appearance of small buds that will become arms. The umbilical cord has now formed.

Milk teeth buds are present.

7 weeks[6]

The baby's face and brain are growing. At around 43 days,[7] brain waves can be recorded, and a few days later, the baby starts generating voluntary movements of the body.

8 weeks

Except for the lungs and the brain, all the organs are complete and functioning. The stomach produces digestive juices. The liver manufactures blood cells. The lower limb buds now take on the appearance of paddles. Fingers have begun to configure. The nose and upper lip have now formed. The baby is now made up of about one billion cells. The baby is now called a foetus.

9 weeks

The baby's fingernails are forming; the baby's thumb is sucked. Elbows and toes are visible. Eyelids and external ears form. The umbilical cord is detectable.

10 weeks

The baby can bend his or her elbows. Toes and fingers no longer have their webbing; they become longer.

11 weeks

By this time, the baby makes facial expressions, including smiling. The baby's taste buds are now functioning. The baby now breathes in amniotic fluid, which happens until birth. Red blood cells are starting to form in the baby's liver. By the end of the eleventh week, the baby's outer genitals will begin developing into a penis or clitoris and labia majora.

12 weeks

The baby's fingernails appear; the intestines are in the abdomen. The baby is capable of kicking, turning over, clenching a fist and opening his or her mouth.

Second Trimester

13 weeks

The baby starts to produce urine. Bones begin to harden. Red blood cells are developing in the bone marrow.

14 weeks

The baby starts to swallow small portions of amniotic fluid which enters the stomach. The kidneys begin to work.

15 weeks

Scalp pattern develops

17 weeks

Around this time, the baby's eyes can move slowly. His or her limb movements are becoming more coordinated. The baby can perform somersaults. The baby will slowly move his or her arms to cover the eyes, if a very bright light is shone on the mother's abdomen. Likewise, the baby will respond to very loud music by covering the ears.

Toenails start developing. The baby's heart now pumps approximately 100 pints of blood daily. The baby becomes more lively, flipping and rolling around in the amniotic sac.

18 weeks

The baby may hear sounds.

19 weeks

In female babies, the uterus and vaginal canal are developing.

20 weeks

The pregnancy is now half complete. The baby is sleeping and waking; his or her senses are sensitive enough for the baby to be awakened by noise or the mother's own movements.

21 weeks

The baby can now suck his or her thumb.

22 weeks

The baby's hair and eyebrows are now detectable. Around this time, the lungs are developing and are capable of absorbing oxygen and eliminating carbon dioxide.

23 weeks

Formation of ridges in the soles of the feet and the palms of the hands. These will later form the basis of footprints and fingerprints respectively. The baby might start hiccupping.

25 weeks

The baby might be able to respond to the mother's voice and movement. During most of the baby's sleeping time there is rapid eye movement, while the eyelids remain closed.

26 weeks

The baby is now composed of about 300 billion cells. Hair is growing on the head. Eyelashes appear.

27 weeks

The baby gains fat. The nervous system continues to develop in maturity.

Third Trimester

28 weeks

Eyelashes have formed and the eyelids can partly open.

29 weeks

The baby can stretch and kick.

30 weeks

The baby's eyes can now open broadly, and he or she might have a head of hair at this point.

31 weeks

The lungs are quickly developing, but from 28 weeks many premature babies are able to breathe spontaneously and independent of the mother.

32 weeks

Toenails are detectable.

33 weeks

The baby's pupils can alter in size, in response to stimulus from light.

35 weeks

The baby is now curled up in the uterus, with legs bent towards the chest. The baby's movements can be clearly seen externally. If the baby is a boy, his testicles are beginning to descend from his abdomen into his scrotum.

36 weeks

The lungs are fully developed. The baby's digestive system is complete, and if he or she is born now, feeding can happen. Babies are able to digest milk from much earlier – from about 24 weeks. They are not able to feed by mouth safely until about 36 weeks.

37 weeks

The baby's head might begin lowering into the mother's pelvis, in preparation for birth.

38 weeks

Labour can begin at any time.

40 weeks

Full term gestation occurs between 37 and 42 weeks, at which point the baby is born.

Sources used:

Human Life International

The Miracle of Fetal Development, by Brian Clowes, PhD https://www.hli.org/resources/miracle-fetal-development/

National Health Service

https://www.nhs.uk/conditions/pregnancy-and-baby/pregnancy-week-by-week/

Mayo Clinic (USA)
First Trimester

https://www.mayoclinic.org/healthy-lifestyle/pregnancy-week-by-week/in-depth/prenatal-care/art-20045302

Second Trimester

https://www.mayoclinic.org/healthy-lifestyle/pregnancy-week-by-week/in-depth/fetal-development/art-20046151

Third Trimester

https://www.mayoclinic.org/healthy-lifestyle/pregnancy-week-by-week/in-depth/fetal-development/art-20045997

Endnotes

---

[1] This refers to post-conceptual age.

[2] This refers to post-conceptual age.

[3] This refers to post-conceptual age.

[4] This is at 8 weeks, post-menstrual age.

[5] This is 5 ½ weeks post-menstrual or 3½ weeks post conceptual age.

[6] This refers to post-menstrual age.

[7] This refers to post-menstrual age.